Le Rugbyman

Le Rugbyman

Kees Meeuws'
Season in the South of France

with Heather Kidd

Hodder Moa

National Library of New Zealand Cataloguing-in-Publication Data

Meeuws, Kees, 1974-
Le rugbyman : Kees Meeuws' season in the south of France /
Kees Meeuws with Heather Kidd. 1st ed.
ISBN 1-86971-024-X
1. Meeuws, Kees, 1974- 2. Rugby Union football players—New
Zealand—Biography. 3. Rugby Union football—France. 4. Rugby
Union football—New Zealand. I. Kidd, Heather, 1954- II. Title.
796.333092—dc 22

A Hodder Moa Book
Published in 2005 by Hachette Livre NZ Ltd
4 Whetu Place, Mairangi Bay
Auckland, New Zealand

Text © Kees Meeuws 2005
The moral rights of the authors have been asserted.
Design and format © Hachette Livre NZ Ltd 2005

All rights reserved. No part of this publication may be reproduced or transmitted in any form or by any means, electronic or mechanical, including photocopying, recording, or any information storage and retrieval system, without permission in writing from the publisher.

Designed and produced by Hachette Livre NZ Ltd
Printed by PrintLink, Wellington, New Zealand

Front and back cover: Fotopress

To my wife and best friend Juanita. Without you none of this would have been possible — you are my world.

Contents

	Writer's Note	8
1	Decision Time	9
2	Early Days	19
3	To France	33
4	Game On	47
5	Spooked	59
6	Christmas is Coming	81
7	Eat, Drink and Be Merry	97
8	A New Year	113
9	Back to Work	129
10	Art	145
11	A Hunting We Will Go	159
12	Spring in the Air	167
13	Getting Away from it All	175
14	Trials and Tribulations	187
15	The Good, the Bad and the Ugly	197
16	Season's End	209
	About the Writer	221

Writer's Note

Kees and I began work on his diary in October last year, a month before he left for France. During those rather frantic few weeks, he managed to find the time to sit down and talk about, in particular, his early years growing up in west Auckland and his All Black career.

There is no doubt Kees' decision to quit the All Blacks and move to France was influenced by the fluidity of the coaching situation in New Zealand. During our meetings Kees talked about his unease with what he regarded as the knee-jerk reaction of the NZRU in recent years to its coaching staff when expectations of on-field success were not achieved.

To me, it seemed the experiences of his friend Ron Cribb, selected by Wayne Smith only to be rejected by John Mitchell, served as the catalyst for Kees deciding to look to a rugby career outside New Zealand. Even the appointment of Graham Henry as All Black coach in late 2003 did not ease Kees' concerns, especially given that Henry's initial appointment was for a two-year term.

Wanting job security, Kees decided to take his rugby talent offshore. That Henry has recently had his tenure extended is a move Kees will approve of. Does it make him regret his decision? Read this book ... the answer is very clear.

Heather Kidd
Auckland
18 May 2005

1
Decision Time

C'est fait. It's done. 8 October 2004. I've signed a contract with rugby club Castres Olympique. In the stroke of a pen, moving to France has become a reality. Tonight, against Otago, I will pull on the Auckland jersey and run out onto Eden Park for the last time. And I'll be doing so with no regrets.

I expect some people will think I'm crazy for choosing to walk away from the All Blacks and Auckland. But it's not a decision I've made lightly; indeed, it has taken five years to get to this point. Back in 1999, during the World Cup campaign, the All Blacks spent a few days in Cannes. Sure, our focus was on rugby but I couldn't help noticing the locals and the way they embraced life. What's that saying? It goes something along the lines of working to live rather than living to work. The French seemed such a happy people; and the other aspect was their language — it really intrigued me.

It always has. The idea of one day making the move to France to play rugby placed itself firmly in my mind.

These days, playing offshore is an option for most rugby professionals. Although some of my best mates have gone to Japan I couldn't envisage myself enjoying a move there. Neither could I see myself joining a club in an English-speaking country. France, with its people, language and culture, has always been top of my list.

But why go now? According to media reports, if there's one player from the 2004 All Black squad being touted as a certainty for Graham Henry's assault on the next World Cup, it is me. Via the grapevine I've heard that he believes I have the potential to go through to the 2007 campaign. Of course such talk is a great confidence booster for me but the big word as far as I'm concerned is 'potential'. Graham can't guarantee me a place in the side any more than I can guarantee my form.

Another major concern for me at this time is that there are absolutely no guarantees Graham will remain in the New Zealand Rugby Union's employ long term. If he doesn't do well against the Lions I'll be surprised if people aren't calling for his head. That's the mentality of the NZRU and also of many New Zealanders — the 'this coach failed, let's get a new one, and maybe he can help us win the World Cup' type of logic. John Mitchell's term showed that, rather than the union persisting with one coach and letting him have a four-year reign, seeing what sort of team he can build-up and develop during that time, the coach's tenure is instead to be totally driven by results. The track record from recent eras for coaches of All Black teams lasting in the job isn't good. In fact it's scary.

I became an All Black in 1998 and during my seven years in the team played under four coaches: John Hart, Wayne

Decision Time

Smith, John Mitchell and Graham Henry. Bottom line: I didn't want a fifth, especially one who might find me surplus to his requirements.

Il est regrettable que nous ne syons pas capables de trouver un solution. It's regrettable that we seem incapable of finding a solution. This year I was coming out of contract and into renegotiating terms with the NZRU. In financial terms their offer was great — I was really happy with it — but from my point of view it lacked long-term security. I spoke to my agent, Wellington-based Rob Brady, and instructed him to explain my situation to the NZRU — that I'm a family man and as such need an income that's assured. I asked them to guarantee me 80 per cent of my contract potential. Put simply, as a professional rugby player in New Zealand, and as an All Black, your income is calculated in a series of percentages. Making the All Blacks is worth 40.5 per cent and then there is 43.5 per cent for inclusion in a Super 12 side. The other 16 per cent comes from NPC selection.

Within the All Black payment schedule, payment is broken up into three sections: domestic test series, Tri-Nations and the end-of-year tour. Each section is calculated on the time/days spent with each section. For example, if there are 100 days to the All Black season, 40 days for the domestic tests would equate to 40 per cent of your payments, 35 days for the Tri Nations is worth 35 per cent and the end-of-year tour would be 25 days for 25 per cent of your payments. There is a payment made to those All Blacks not initially selected and who then make the side for what is left of the season — along with those who are called in to cover injuries. Therefore, in order to receive your full payment you have to be selected for all campaigns (unless, as may happen with the end-of-year tour, you are told specifically to stay home). If you don't make the All Blacks or you get dropped during the season, your earning capacity likewise drops to 59.5 per cent of its potential.

Imagine trying to plan your life around that word: 'potential'. You have the 'potential' to earn $350,000 — *but* — and it's a sizeable 'but', just over 40 per cent of that, $150,000, relies on your making the All Blacks. And earning that $150,000 depends on the player continuing to win All Black selection over an entire 12-month period.

The NZRU knows many of the young players aren't going to make the final cut but they talk up the biggest figure, get the guys to sign contracts and, therefore, no matter what, the players *have* to stay in New Zealand.

I don't want to be locked into a contract that's so heavily biased in favour of the employer. The NZRU's product is the All Blacks, and as far as I'm concerned they don't seem to give a shit about the players. I think their mentality is, 'If he goes, so what, we'll easily get someone to replace him'. In my opinion, the aim should be to produce a winning team, but the union's current mindset is not conducive to building one; it's too much 'them against us' and there's no feeling that players and union are working together towards a common goal.

The NZRU flew me to Wellington to meet with the contracts' team and Graham Henry but there were never any formal financial discussions. No one ever asked what it would take to keep me in New Zealand.

The possibility that Graham Henry might not win tenure through to the next World Cup concerns me big time. I've seen the

Decision Time

fallout from a change of coaches. A good friend of mine, Ron Cribb, went from hero to zero almost overnight. Ron was first choice No 8 when Wayne Smith was All Black coach and during that time Ron signed a five-year contract with the NZRU. But suddenly Wayne was gone, John Mitchell took over and he rated Ron as seventh or eighth choice, thus making it clear that Ron would never make the All Blacks while Mitch was coach. It illustrates the point that there's no job security even when players are supposedly at the top, and just how quickly they can suddenly find themselves on the outer — trapped — locked in to a contract. Luckily, Ron got out of his. But it came at a price; he had to fight like a dog to win his release and was forced to stand down from rugby for a year.

I didn't like the way the NZRU contract was going to lock me in. Sure, I appreciate the positive, that the All Black coaching team have faith in me and think I could be there for the next World Cup. But I can't return the vote of confidence and sign a contract certain that Graham Henry, Wayne Smith and Steve Hansen will be the coaching triumvirate in 2007.

But playing for the All Blacks is not just about the coaching staff. I have to take a good hard look at myself too and I've come to the conclusion that I don't believe I can make the next World Cup. The schedule of Super 12, NPC, the All Blacks campaign plus an end-of-year tour were lacking in appeal. Go away on a tour and it's early December before you're home and then you have to be back into Super 12 training a month later, which means you've got only one month to get any niggles right. Also, you have to maintain fitness levels for that month; there's no opportunity to relax and get fat(!). Quite frankly, after three back-to-back seasons I don't believe I can do six in a row. I need a break.

Le Rugbyman

Vous devez décider de ce qui compte le plus pour vous. You must get your priorities right. It took what was to be my last campaign with the All Blacks to cement that thought. I came home mentally and physically exhausted from the Tri Nations. I'd been playing virtually non-stop for three years and I'd reached the point where I didn't want to play rugby any more. Ever. Playing rugby at the top level in New Zealand takes you away from your family. My youngest daughter had been born at the beginning of the year and when I got back from the Tri Nations I found myself thinking, 'Who is this little kid?' I'd scarcely spent any time with Inez for the seven months of her life. Sure, I'd get to see her on weekends or for a couple of days during a week, but with all the travelling, training and playing in the name of rugby, I realised I was missing out on the best years of my life with my young children. It brought me up short. My family means the world to me.

I've played 42 tests for the All Blacks since my debut in 1998, 45 games in all, and over the years the game has given me some awesome memories — the good, the bad and the ugly. Equalling and then breaking the world record for tries scored by a prop playing international rugby were brilliant moments. At the other end of the scale, losing the 1999 World Cup semi-final to France was a heartbreaker. But what happened to the players, the abuse they suffered when they returned to New Zealand, made the disappointment at not attaining our goal even worse. The 2003 World Cup campaign was another nadir. During my time as an All Black, not winning the Bledisloe Cup until 2003 was a constant frustration, but that made the eventual winning of it, and then going on to retain the trophy, huge highlights.

Once we won that game in Wellington in July 2004, beating

Decision Time

Australia 16–7, it was as if a huge weight had been lifted from our shoulders. But just to prove the point that there's never any room for complacency in competitive sport, the wheels fell off during our Tri Nations campaign and we crashed to last place, only the second time we've finished behind Australia and South Africa since the tournament's inception. Back in 1998 the All Blacks lost every game, so I guess we could take some solace in managing a couple of wins.

But there was no getting away from the fact that it was tough going, on and off the field. By the time I got back home to Auckland my thinking was: 'If this is what it's going to be like every year through to the next World Cup, I don't think I can do this.' My wife Juanita thought I was having a mental breakdown because I just sat on the couch for two days and didn't move.

I decided I had to get out of Auckland, so a couple of weeks prior to the NPC, I headed down to Dunedin. There, I could get right away from rugby, chill out, do some pig hunting, clear my head and work out what to do with my life, hopefully reaching a decision that was going to be in the best interests of me and my family.

It took me two weeks to want to pull on my rugby boots again. Maybe it was fate, but during my stay in Dunedin I got the call from Castres, a club that plays in the French first division, Le Championnat de France, and also in the much-vaunted European Cup. The club has a proud history: champion of France 1993, finalist in 1995, and several-times-qualifier for the Heineken Cup competition.

Earlier in the season and dealing through my agent, I'd put out a few feelers with a view to playing overseas. Two French clubs, neighbouring arch-rivals Toulouse and Castres, had been in contact. Initially, Toulouse was keen and negotiations seemed to be going well. But the next thing I heard was that they'd signed another player.

I was disappointed but tried to be philosophical. Surely something else would come along?

We also talked with Castres but negotiations stalled over the problem of timing. The club wanted me there in August, but because of my contractual obligations to New Zealand I wasn't available to make a move until later in the year. They were very keen to sign me and apparently tried to reach me the Friday night prior to the test against the Pacific Islanders. But I had my mobile switched off and it was left to Rob Brady to do the negotiations. It didn't seem, though, that patience was one of the virtues of the Castres club.

According to Rob they gave him a deadline of 6 am New Zealand time the morning of the match, 10 July, to have a contract signed and faxed back to France. There was no way we could meet those deadlines and it didn't seem as though there was a solution available that could be satisfactory to both parties.

Encore une chance. A second chance. It was something of a surprise, a nice one too as it turned out, when Castres rang to say they'd had a re-think and were willing to bring me over at the end of November with a view to my being ready to play for them from December. I'd be going as what they term their 'joker', a replacement for a supposedly injured player. It is the only way I can arrive during the actual season because under French regulations players have to be signed and available to play for their club by August.

My interest was sparked. Could this be the opportunity I'd been waiting for? I spoke with Juanita and then called Brad Fleming, a former Otago Highlanders player and New Zealand Sevens rep who's been playing for Castres since the start of the 2004–2005 season. Brad is one of a number of foreigners at the club, which

Decision Time

apparently includes players from England, Ireland, Argentina, South Africa and, of course, New Zealand — a regular United Nations it seems, and with a few Frenchmen thrown in as well. Brad says most of the boys speak English so there should be little, if any, problem of a language barrier.

But if I'm going to move to France I'll want to learn the lingo. Hopefully after a couple of weeks talking to me in English I will be wanting them to converse in French. All the calls should be the same — just in another language, and there aren't so many that they'll be hard to pick up. And getting penalised is certainly the same in any country! Brad talks me through the club's training schedule: once a day three times a week and twice a day on Mondays plus one other. Trainings last for about two and a half hours and the forwards do a lot of scrums. He says the club is one of the more professional sides in France and they train as such — although it's nothing like New Zealand and I'll be in for a shock.

The good news is that there are no lengthy trips away. For away matches, generally the team flies or buses out the day or evening prior to a game and returns home straight after the match. Brad adds that the town is great, on the small side, probably similar in size to Invercargill, and that the people are friendly. Should I decide to uproot my family and myself for foreign shores, he reckons we'll love it.

What to do? Should I sign another contract with New Zealand and hope everything goes according to *my* plan, the one that involves no changes of coach in the New Zealand set up, no drop-off in my form and me getting my enthusiasm back? Or should I walk away to realise a long-held dream of living and playing overseas? We'd be living in France — a country Juanita and I have such fond memories of — and having the opportunity to make trips to Paris, a city that held us spellbound and has become our Mecca.

We would be able to immerse ourselves in a foreign culture, living it rather than just passing through, and I could continue to play rugby and build a secure financial future for my family. I've talked to a lot of mates who've lived and played in foreign countries and they reckon it's got great advantages for the family unit. Juanita and I are very keen about this aspect.

For 18 months I've battled with these options, even making lists of the pros and cons (and where the reasons for going far outnumber the reasons for staying), and the day I always knew would come, when I would leave my All Black career behind.

The 2004 season has had it all — a real mix of fortunes on the pitch for the team, going from the high of beating England twice but then slumping to last place in the Tri Nations. However, on a personal level, I've been going great, back in the All Blacks' starting lineup and being told, 'You're playing awesome rugby', even making the switch from tighthead to loosehead without any real problems.

Funnily enough, my success reinforces an old saying I've held dear throughout my All Black career — that you're a peacock one day and a feather duster the next. I want to leave the All Blacks as a peacock and not as a feather duster. And so, after weighing up all the options, I've decided now is the perfect time to quit.

2
Early Days

La vie. Life. Mid-October 2004. It's all about taking on challenges and that's what I'm raring to do. The thought of moving to the other side of the world, to the south of France, is exciting, and hey, if it isn't going to be challenging too, what's the point in going?

Maybe it's in the blood. Certainly, my father was a man who relished a challenge. Cornelius Antonius Meeuws was his name. He was born in the Netherlands and came to New Zealand in the 1950s after doing a stint with the Dutch airforce in Indonesia. He worked in supplies. Like many of his peers, he was given the opportunity to emigrate to New Zealand and when he arrived he went straight into the construction business, working on hydro dam schemes throughout the country. Despite being in his early twenties when he got here, he never lost his thick Dutch accent, and, because he worked in the construction industry environment, the first words of

English he learned to speak became words he used quite frequently in normal speech — and they weren't very pleasant ones! My old man could swear like a trooper. Although, having said that, he did manage to moderate his language as he got older.

Dad was based in Mangakino (north-west of Taupo) for quite a while and that's where he met my mother, Rebecca. Her father, Jack Judah, was my father's foreman and my mum, if I remember correctly, worked in the local dairy, which is where Dad met her. It's quite a funny story. Apparently my mother was promised to someone else (that was the custom with many Maori back in those days) but she started seeing my dad and became pregnant to him. When my grandfather found out I gather he was quite keen to go and kill my father! But fortunately it all worked out for the best. One of my uncles acted as the go-between and settled everyone down and Mum and Dad were allowed to marry — two people from vastly different cultures — she from Ngati Maru and Ngati Whare and of the Parahauraki iwi, and my father from The Hague. I might be a Dutch-Maori mix — I'm fortunate enough to carry European and New Zealand passports — but I consider myself pure Kiwi, a New Zealander and proud of it.

My parents continued to live in Mangakino during the early years of their marriage and then moved to Auckland when my brother and sister, Johan and Roberta, were about five and four years old respectively. My parents built a house at Glendene, West Auckland, and that's where I was born and brought up, the second youngest in a family of seven. We're pretty spread out age-wise. Johan is 21 years older than me, and then there are the four girls, Roberta, 20 years my senior, followed by Sylvia, Gloria and Monique. I was born when Monique was six years old, and the final addition to our family was

Early Days

my brother, Johnny, who is two years younger than I am. Sure, the boys are well outnumbered by the females but I wouldn't have it any other way. They all spoil me because I'm one of the babies of the family. I loved our life in West Auckland and am living proof of the sentiment, 'once a Westie, always a Westie'. I may never reside in the area again but its spirit lives within me.

Mum was really sporty and her main loves were netball, basketball and badminton. People keep telling me she was a talented sportswoman but once she had her family it was us kids who became her main focus. She was happy to act as the chauffeur, taking us to our sports and cheering us on from the sidelines.

Douloureux. Loss. But Mum died when I was 10 years old. It was a terrible time in my life and I don't remember it well. I think I've blocked a lot out because it's simply too painful. There is much about my younger years I don't remember, that I learned to shut out. Sometimes I look at photos taken during those years, and although I can recall what was happening around the time the pictures were taken, my memories beyond that are pretty hazy.

Belonging to a strong family unit, though, helped pull us through Mum's death. At the time, only Monique, Johnny and I were still living at home with Dad; everyone else had either started their own families or they were out in the world doing their own thing. But we always had good support and it got us through that toughest of times.

C'est resté incertain jusq'au bout. Touch and go. But the tough times were not over. Within a year I would be facing a major health scare, one that almost cost me half my leg. It all started innocently enough. I'd got the chance to be involved with a new family drama,

Steel Riders, produced by South Pacific Pictures. It was pretty much about a group of kids who ride BMX bikes and stuff up a robbery. I was out practising on my bike at the BMX track and I cut my ankle. Although the cut was deep I decided it was nothing more serious than a little scratch and I didn't take much notice of it. I was soon forced to, however.

One evening I suddenly collapsed. Dad put me to bed. He was worried and kept an eye on me and then, next morning, I collapsed again. I remember Dad being in a real panic and he took me immediately to see our GP, Dr Stone.

I'm a bit hazy about my exact symptoms but they obviously rang an alarm bell with the doctor. Apparently a couple of months earlier he'd had a similar case and that patient was diagnosed as suffering from osteomyelitis, an infection of the bone. I was sent to hospital for further tests and the results came back positive.

Immediately, I was hooked up to an IV drip and given high-dosage antibiotics. I seemed to have tubes poking in all over my body. For four days there were no signs of improvement. My raging fever wasn't abating and my condition was deteriorating. The doctors told my father that amputating my right leg from the knee down was the only hope of saving me.

It fell to Dad to explain the gravity of the situation to me and I think it was one of the most difficult conversations we were ever to have. I was overwhelmed and I think he was too. I have a vivid recollection of telling my father that there was no way the doctors were to be allowed to take my leg off. I pleaded with him to make the doctors give me more time, even just one day.

Poor Dad kept trying to tell me that amputation was the only option. I can understand his point of view. He wanted his son to

Early Days

live and if that meant I was missing half a limb, to him that was infinitely preferable to watching me die. It was just a year since Mum had died, after all.

But with all the confidence of an 11 year old, I was determined that my leg was to stay firmly attached to my body. I even contemplated running away from hospital in order to make my point. In hindsight, I probably wouldn't have got very far. But I wasn't scared. All the machinery that I was hooked up to didn't faze me and I refused to contemplate the loss of a limb. Deep down, I just knew everything would be okay.

And 24 hours later my inner faith was proved correct. The antibiotics started to take effect, my fever subsided and I was beginning to feel more like my old self. The medical staff told my father they were amazed to see such a dramatic change in such a short space of time.

I spent another week in hospital and when I was allowed home it was with two 'buckets' of antibiotics. I had to take 12 tablets each day, six in the morning and the other six at night, for the next six months. Although my foot was in a cast I didn't let that stop me from playing rugby and bull-rush and generally getting involved in all the activities that appeal to a young boy. Poor Dad was forever taking me to the hospital to have the cast replaced — I think we worked out I was having a new one put on every 10 days for a while. Fibreglass casts proved ineffectual too. I kept snapping them. There must have been a collective sigh of relief from my father and staff at the hospital when the plaster came off for good after three months. And three months after that I was given the all clear.

I have often wondered what life would have been like if my lower leg had been amputated. The thought was certainly uppermost in my mind when I went to watch the 2000 Paralympic Games in Sydney.

As I watched the athletes, I acknowledged that losing a limb would not have dulled my competitive spirit, that somehow my passion for sport would have continued to exist, albeit on a different playing field. Love of competition is an intrinsic part of me; I get that from my mother.

The passion Mum had for sport has most certainly lived on through her family. Johan played rugby at club level. Sylvia was the best sportswoman in our family and she represented New Zealand in softball. Then, just as Sylvia was winding down, Monique was on her way up, and she played softball for the New Zealand under-19s and at the top level in Auckland. Because my sisters played it was only natural for me to think softball was the best sport in the world. Naturally I wanted to be a part of it and I started playing when I was about eight years old.

Rugby à quinze. Rugby union. It was at about this time that I got into rugby. We used to play bull-rush all the time with the kids in our street, some of whom were three to four years older than me and it's fair to say I could hold my own against them. One of the kids' fathers was coach at Te Atatu and he asked if I'd like to come down and join the club and he gave me a letter to take home to my father. Dad was happy to give his permission and he joined up my younger brother and me with the club. By the time I was 10 years old I was also playing for my school team at Tirimoana Primary and I like to think I was pretty useful.

I know it won't come as a surprise to anyone but, yes, I was a big kid for my age, a 'well-built fellow' as they say. Rugby wasn't my only sport either. I was into athletics and wrestling for a good few years. I joined the Glendene Athletics Club in my fourth form

— a big sporting year for me as it turned out — and my events were shot put, long jump and the 100 metres. The heavier I got, the less competitive I became in the long jump and 100 metres, but I continued to take a serious part in shot put competition through to my seventh form year. I set a new Kelston Boys High School Junior shot record in 1988 with a throw of 11.72 m and it stood for 16 years, only being broken in 2004. In 1990 I threw 13.65 m to set a new Intermediate shot record. That one still has my name on it.

In my final year at school, 1992, I won the North Island champs at shot put and then went to the New Zealand Secondary Schools' championships where I was placed third with a throw of 13.58 m. First place went to Rodney Hogg of Southland Boys High School, who threw 15.10 m. At least I had the satisfaction of beating one Daryl Gibson. His throw of 12.5 m earned him seventh place. He did better in the discus competition, coming third.

We were competing in exalted company as it turns out. Beatrice Faumuina (world championship and Commonwealth Games gold-medal winner in discus) was already a leading light in field events, winning the senior girls shot put and discus events, with Bernice Mene second to her in both. And it turns out that my Castres team-mate, Brad Fleming, was also competing at the time. He finished fifth in the 100 metres.

Looking back, I wish I'd trained harder for those champs but they were held at the end of the year around Bursary exam time and I'd sacrificed my training to study. What grates is that my best throw at the North Island's would have won me the national championships.

I was also part of the school 4 x 100 metres relay team that ran in the final of the New Zealand school championships that year.

Le Rugbyman

But rugby remained my first sporting love. From the outset I played prop and only deviated briefly from that position and during high school I made the cut for the Kelston BHS First XV in my fourth form year. I worked my way up through the representative team ranks, playing for the Auckland under-13s and then, twice, for the Auckland under-14s (I always played a year ahead of my age), then the under-15s, and went on to make every representative team since. At New Zealand level, I made the under-17s in 1991 and again played my way through all the grades up to and including the All Blacks.

History will record Kees Junior Meeuws as Kelston Boys' High School's third All Black. The first was none other than Va'aiga Tuigamala, a.k.a. Inga the Winger, and the second was Jason Hewett. Inga, five years older than me, was one of my heroes when I was growing up, a role model both as a rugby player and as a human being, and the fact he'd been to Kelston Boys' was one of the reasons I chose to go there too.

En pleine forme. In great form. And like Inga, I think it's fair to say I made an impact at high school level. During my third form, I enjoyed a great season with the under-15s. We played in the 3M tournament, held in Whangarei, and I was in outstanding form. However, it almost worked against me because after that the school was keen to look after me, saying, 'We want to develop you for the First XV.' Of course, being young and confident I was raring to go, quite certain that I didn't need to waste time being minded through any so-called 'development' stage. All I wanted was an opportunity to show the coaches I was ready to mix it with the big guys — and anyway, wasn't I big for my age? But that fact cut no ice with the

Early Days

school coaches. In their considered opinion I was probably still a little too light for the First XV front row. But I wasn't about to give up. There was a trial match to select the First XV squad scheduled to be held in Whangarei and although I knew I wasn't in the reckoning for a first team place I persuaded the coaches to give me a trial, saying, 'Put me on and I'll show you.' I got the nod but it was as a blindside flanker.

My persuasive abilities probably owe more to my on-the-field activities than any verbal talents. At the time I was also wrestling and a by-product of that discipline was a substantial increase in my strength. I could really tackle. I think it's fair to say that during the trial I tackled my butt off. I mightn't have known what I was doing playing blindside but I ran around tackling everything that moved, diving in rucks and generally making a real nuisance of myself. Fortunately, the coaches liked what they saw and I made the First XV during my fourth form. The following year I played a combination of prop and blindside flanker for the school and then, what with the wrestling, weight training and filling out a bit more, I slotted back into the front row fulltime. My days as a flanker were well and truly over.

And my days of wrestling were also done. I loved the sport and wrestled for the school, which was renowned for its strong wrestling squad, and I also belonged to the Kelston Wrestling Club. We trained Tuesdays and Thursdays — sound familiar? — but as well as training times, the timetable clashes between rugby and wrestling tournaments meant something had to give.

Un objectif dans la vie. A purpose in life. In the end it wasn't a hard decision. Rugby was my passion and I'd made up my mind to pursue it as far as I could. I wanted to be an All Black. But I had to temper that goal with realism, accept that it could turn out to be a goal too far and not make my quest the be-all and end-all of life. Remember this is in pre-professional rugby days. I decided I would push the boundaries of my rugby as far as I could and see what might eventuate while trying to remain clear-headed. I knew rugby players had to make a living as well as playing sport and it was important I set myself up with an education so that if my rugby tipped over I'd have something to fall back on. I made up my mind to go to university.

Maybe Graham Henry's thinking was similar to mine — but in reverse. He was principal of Kelston Boys' during my years at the school and he became Auckland coach in 1992, which was my final year at school. During my time at Kelston, Graham didn't have a lot to do with our First XV. We were doing all right with the coaches we had, especially when I was first in the team. During that 1989 season we won the national First XV Invitational Tournament, beating Wesley College 22–19 in the final.

But Graham's influence was always there, of that there's no doubt. If we hit a hard patch he'd come in and help out and he got some of the Auckland boys to take us through coaching sessions. But his influence was more indirect than direct. I can totally see where he was coming from when, in 1993, he left Kelston to concentrate fulltime on being a coach. Of course our paths have crossed several times since and it's been really good to have that history — a rapport and respect for each other. I appreciate that Graham treats me like a man and not a boy. Too many coaches treat players like boys. I have a theory that teachers make better coaches than ex-players. Teachers know how to handle different types of people whereas an ex-player tends to treat everyone the same. And we're not. Some people can handle being growled at and there are other guys who need to be wrapped in cottonwool or have their egos propped up in order to get them to perform to their best. I think teachers-turned-coaches make better judgement calls on which people need what attention, due to experiences gained in the classroom where they've had to deal with people from a range of backgrounds, from the troublesome kid with problems at home to the well-behaved ones. Generally, they know how to get the best out of people and, in my mind, it makes them better coaches. With someone like Graham it is refreshing to be able to speak my mind, man to man.

I'd like to think that Graham will remain in coaching as long as he wishes but with his background in education it must be reassuring for him to know he can always return to teaching if his coaching career falls over.

Maison à vendre. House for sale. It's late October and Juanita and I have had to make some tough decisions. Okay, making the move to France was *the* biggest, but because we intend to be away for a minimum of three years we have to make some choices in relation to our properties. We have two houses, one in Auckland and another in Dunedin, so should we sell one or both? In the end the decision is pretty easy. I may be a born-and-bred Aucklander but I don't see a future for myself that would involve living in the City of Sails. I love the South Island and I love Dunedin. It's a city with a small-town ambience and the best of mother nature close at hand. You've got 27 surf breaks in a seven-kilometre radius, the possibility of hunting 20 minutes from your front door, and the ski fields within a two-and-a-half to three-hour drive. There's fishing on your back doorstep and all the lakes and mountains nearby in which to go exploring. It's such a beautiful part of New Zealand. Yes, it can be cold, but I'd rather be cold than hot. At least you can dress up for cooler climates.

Auckland can be so incredibly humid and if you decide to go to the beach to cool off you're likely to find every other Aucklander has had the same idea and you're all there fighting for a bit of towel space. In Dunedin you'd be pretty lucky if it was ever warm enough to go sunbathing!

In 2001, Juanita and I built a house in Dunedin. We lived in it for just 13 months before we made the move to Auckland when I got the offer to join the Blues. It's a lovely house and, ironically, quite French in style; it's another incentive for us to eventually settle back down south.

Our house in Greenhithe sold without going on the market, which was a huge plus, but it doesn't make the actual shifting out process any easier. We're moving out in three days' time, leaving here for a hotel room in the central city where we'll be based for 10 days before heading south to say our farewells to friends and family in Dunedin.

It's safe to say chaos reigns. Juanita has been ill, struck down by the virus that affected so many this winter and now Eva is unwell. The state of the house mirrors our feelings exactly — it's a jumble. For my family and me, our emotions are in a whirl; all around us our household effects are stacked up, lining the walls and spilling out into the entranceway, some boxed and ready to go into storage. Other things, our most prized possessions, are bound in bubble-wrap and cardboard and ready to make the long haul to France.

Our treasured dining-room suite is making the trip. The table is a massive piece of furniture that can easily seat eight around it. The mechanics of our social life, as the smaller family unit or with bigger get-togethers, revolve around food. We love entertaining and I don't see that changing when we're living in France; in fact, hopefully, we'll be doing more of it. It could be a good way to learn the language and I want to show the French some Kiwi cuisine and demonstrate my cooking skills. But even those have been put on hold for the moment because most of our kitchenware is packed and the only usable table is on the deck, part of our outdoor furniture set.

But while I may not be able to keep up to speed with my cooking, I am brushing up on another important aspect of French life: I'm taking French lessons. To date I've had four sessions and I like to think they're going well. I didn't take French at school so I have to start from scratch. My tutor reckons the format for their sentence structure is the hardest thing to master but once you get the gist of that you can get through anything. I know about the *le, la, il* and *elle* — that everything is either male or female. He's also been telling me what the French are like as a people. He says they get really involved in where you come from, so I've got to be able to say, 'I come from here' or 'I live in such-and-such a type of house'; that's the sort of thing they will want to know apparently.

He also said to make sure we have lots of photos from here because the people we meet will want to know where we are from, what sort of vehicles we drive here, what our house looks like, our families, indicators of our way of life. I'm enjoying the lessons and, fingers crossed, think I'm getting there, albeit slowly.

Juanita is probably a lot further ahead than I am and she can certainly understand much of what is being said. She took French at school and when we were in France after the '99 World Cup she did all the talking for us. She even surprised herself with how much she remembered from her school days. She certainly saved my bacon a few times!

Juanita and I have known each other for years but I actually had more to do with her father, Brian Steel, before I got together with his daughter. Steelo, as he's known, is one of my pig-hunting mates from Dunedin. Juanita and I were mates too but it wasn't until she moved away to Auckland in 1998 that I decided *hey, I like you*. We were married in 2000 and have two daughters, Eva, who is three, and 10-month-old Inez. I also have three children from a previous relationship. Javier is 11 years old and he's at my old school, Rangeview Intermediate, and then there are the twins, a boy and girl, Cayne and Tayla, and they are aged nine. It will be a wrench moving so far away from them but we are planning for them to come and spend some time with us in France.

3
To France

L'heure de vérité. The hour of truth. Best laid plans and all that! It's Friday November 5 and I depart for France at 3 pm. It is going to be a hectic day; well, the whole week has been a mad rush since Castres requested, quite forcibly, that I come across earlier than my contract stipulates — which names a date at the end of this month. Initially, I was quite annoyed. Bringing my departure date forward means I don't get to do half the things I'd planned, such as going down to Dunedin and saying my goodbyes to family and friends. It also means Juanita will have to travel alone with two small girls, although the club has indicated it might be willing to fly an extra family member over, return business class, to help her out. Maybe Castres need me there early to cover for an injury or the like. I really don't know, but they're obviously emotional people and at the end of the day you've got to try to please your employer. There's no point in starting off on the wrong foot.

Le Rugbyman

We have an early start to the day. Firstly, it's a matter of organising the girls. Eva is going to the crèche and because Inez is sick, she stays with Juanita while I take my All Black car back to Ford. I spend three-quarters of an hour with the assessor; the car is in mint condition so there are no repair costs. Then it's off to the lawyers to tie up some loose ends and by the time I get back to the hotel it's 11 am and I still need to pack. Because Juanita and the girls will be travelling at a later date I have to take a lot of their luggage to try and make the journey easier on her and the kids. This means I'll be travelling with seven bags instead of my usual three and I'm anticipating this is going to cost a small fortune in excess. It takes me an hour to pack. I have to be at the airport at 1 pm for check-in.

When we arrive at the airport it is to discover that the All Blacks are leaving at around the same time. Although it will be good to catch up with a few boys before I go, I feel a little uncomfortable about seeing management. I'm big on manners and there's a part of me that feels I haven't properly acknowledged how much I appreciate the selectors' faith in me. I worry that my choosing to continue my rugby career overseas could have been construed, wrongly, as my saying, 'Thanks, but no thanks' to the very people who believe in my ability as a player.

My check-in goes smoothly except that it costs $4000 for excess luggage. Ouch! I have 107 kg in total, which pushes me 47 kg over my weight allocation of 60 kg. I hope the club will reimburse me. (I later find out that they will — phew!)

I did see some of my All Black mates and management and it was good to wish them good luck and to have a quick chat. However, I missed most of the team because by the time I'd said all my goodbyes and passed through Customs they'd received their final boarding call.

To France

I quickly discover the difference between travelling as part of a rugby team and going it alone. As I go through Customs they ask if I've paid the departure tax. I haven't. When you travel with a team things like that are taken care of. It's a bit of a wake-up call for me. I need to get out of that mentality. I have to go back out to the BNZ to pay the tax then, second time around, proceed through Departures without any problems.

I run into Tana Umaga and Doug Howlett on the way to the Koru Lounge and wish them all the best and a safe tour, and say that I'll see if I am able to make it to the test in Paris. It feels a bit strange not being a part of the All Blacks yet being at the airport at the same time and departing the country within half an hour of them. But there are no pangs of regret. I'm excited about my future and I'm looking forward to experiencing life in the south of France.

Sur le sol français. On French soil. It is Sunday November 7 and the flight from New Zealand goes well but it is definitely long haul — 33-and-a-half hours in total — 10 hours to Singapore, with a three-and-a-half hour stopover there followed by a 12-and-a-half hour flight to Frankfurt. I have to endure another lengthy stopover, this time it is four-and-a-half hours, and my final flight is a mere two hours to Toulouse. The last leg of this marathon journey is completed on land — a one-hour drive to Castres.

I am pretty tired by the time I arrive at Toulouse airport because I've managed only four hours' sleep during the trip. It is about 11 o'clock when the plane touches down in Toulouse. I am expecting to be met by someone holding a sign saying 'Kees Meeuws' but there is no-one immediately apparent.

First thought: *Shit, I get all the way over here and the French forget to pick me up!* But within five minutes the troops arrive; Patrick Alran, the director of Castres Olympique Rugby, greets me and he's accompanied by two TV news crews. I can't seem to get away from the media. However, getting through Customs proves easy. No-one wants to check any of my vast array of luggage and all that's required is my being asked to sign a few autographs for the rugby-mad Customs officers.

The drive from Toulouse to Castres is amazing. It is picture-postcard perfect, the countryside exactly like the photographs I have seen in books about the south of France. It is everything I've anticipated — and more. We whiz past farmland dotted with amazingly gracious manors or mansions, seemingly built in the middle of nowhere. The small towns we pass through look as if they belong in *le moyen âge*, the Middle Ages. It finally hits me that I'm about to start an experience of a lifetime and how exciting it's going to be.

By the time we arrive in Castres it is 2 pm and I'm starving. Airline food has never really done it for me, even travelling business class. I always need about two-plus meals to touch the sides but now, with my feet back on the ground, I feel rude asking for something to eat. Patrick tells me that in France only a few places serve food or meals after 2 pm, and the same restaurants are open on Sunday because everything else is closed. In Castres that means there are only three choices — McDonald's, a *patisserie* (bakery), and an American-style steak house (Buffalo Grill), a bit like New Zealand's Cobb & Co restaurant chain. So, it's off to Buffalo Grill for a steak. One-and-a-half hours and two bottles of wine later we emerge. I'm quite tired but I don't want to sleep until at least 9 pm because the quicker I can adapt to local time the quicker I'll get over the effects of jet lag.

I am taken to the hotel where I'll be staying for the next week until my family arrives. It's an amazing little boutique hotel with a stairwell that has Romeo and Juliet-type balconies opening up into the foyer, plants hanging off the walls and a glass ceiling to let in natural light. My room is a cosy single room but with a double bed (leopard skin blanket with zebra skin pillows — real porn-set glamour!) and a desk, television, fridge and bathroom. The exposed beams and bricks give some indication as to just how old this place is.

Brad and Adele Fleming arrive a while later. They give me a quick tour of the town and then our first port of call is to a fellow player's house. It's a popular place. He has Sky TV — the English version. A few of the English-speaking boys (two Poms, Paul Volley and Mark Denney), a South African (Jacques Dean) and two Kiwis (Glen Metcalfe who played No 15 for Scotland, plus Brad) have got together to watch the South Africa versus Wales test. For me, it's great to meet players who've experienced what I am about to go through. I hope that listening and talking to them will make the transition much easier for my family and me.

After the game Jacques, Brad, Adele and I set off to have a beer at a pub-café that is owned by two of the players from Castres. We're there less than five minutes when two reporters from the local newspaper bail me up for an interview.

I meet a few of the players that night and I find it tough going. Only a few of them speak pidgin English. After the meet 'n' greet we head to a local restaurant, La Grillade. The owner, Jacques, invited us to dinner the following night. My first impressions are that they seem a friendly bunch.

It is at Jacques' house the next evening where I meet a man who could well be in the running for the title of biggest man in the world. Former French and Castres prop Gerard Cholley is a legend in these parts. Gary Whetton could testify as to this man — there are many photos of Gary, who played for Castres, and Gerard on the walls of La Grillade. Then, as now, it was a favoured meeting place for players from Castres, local or foreign.

On meeting Gerard I can't help but notice the gold chain around his neck. It has a gold rectangular-shaped medallion hanging from it and one corner is a piece of lead. I ask him about it and tell him I'm especially intrigued by the piece of lead.

The story Gerard tells me comes under the 'crazy' category. Apparently, he was in a bar about eight years ago and got into an argument with a local — this, I might add, is not uncommon for the French. However, the local went out to his car, returned with a gun and shot Gerard in the head! Now Gerard is big. And I mean solid — not flabby in the least — and due to all his years of scrummaging and ramming heads with other props, his forehead has thickened to the extent that even a bullet can't penetrate his skull! He says the necklace serves as a reminder to him of how rugby saved his life, thus bringing a whole new meaning to rugby as an institution. I can hear the slogan now: 'Rugby, it *can* save your life.'

Kai time. The meal Jacques has prepared is traditional French. We begin with red wine followed by an *apéritif*, more red wine; caviar and *fromage* (cheese) salad which serves as an entrée; more red wine. Then we move on to the main course, which is roasted *poulet* (chicken) with *légumes* (vegetables), *pommes de terre* (potatoes) and, of course, more red wine. Dessert is a choice of *gâteau* or a pastry. I can't choose between them so I have both. The meal is divine and Jacques informs us that we've been taken on a tour of France — red wine style — beginning in the north of the country and ending in the south. I have a glow on and consider this *tour de France* awesome. For a *digestif*, we are offered a glass of cognac that is more than 200 years old. It comes in a *mathusalem* (a huge bottle) that holds about six litres and costs something in the region of €12,000 (approximately NZ $26,000). It tastes great and packs a punch! Well, regardless of how it tasted (and thank god it was good) you'd force yourself to enjoy it for that price, wouldn't you? I feel privileged to have been invited to have a glass of this cognac. I don't know how much longer it will last. There's only about a litre left.

The dinner, the whole evening, is an excellent experience of French hospitality. I also enjoy the fact that only one of my teammates can translate English to French.

Since that gastronomical experience I've returned to Jacques' restaurant many times and am always satisfied with the kai and his hospitality — despite not being able to communicate with him in any language. The message gets through, however; there are lots of hands and arms flaying, laughter and broad grins. My limited French vocabulary and my favourite French word, 'oui', are getting me by just fine for the time being.

Prêt à tout. Ready for anything. On Monday, just two days after my arrival, I pick up my car. Obviously, I'm expected to know my way around the town. Armed with a dodgy map and some Maori instinct I set off in my smart black Citroën Picasso and get lost. Often!

They say there is no better way to discover a place than by getting lost and I can happily say that after a few hours in the car I think I have this place sewn up.

The biggest challenge is remembering to drive on the right-hand side of the road. Apart from this it's pretty simple. The rules are similar to New Zealand's but the French don't appear to have much regard for rules — hence all the roundabouts — but on the plus side they are polite and to date I've not come across any road rage. I feel I can speak with some authority on this subject. I'm sure I must have stirred up some of the locals while getting lost in this town but, fortunately, to date no one's taken obvious offence. I haven't been shot at for starters!

Le rugby. On the rugby front, Monday's also my first day having a good look around the club and getting to meet the team. Our training facilities are on one side of the town, about a 10-minute drive on the main road to Toulouse, and where we play, at Stadium Pierre Antoine, is on the other. The stadium, which holds about 8000 people, takes its name from a saint and its formal name is Holy Stade Pierre Antoine. A former player for Castres, and with a name not dissimilar to the saint, one Jean-Pierre Antoine, met an untimely end during the 1956–57 season. Apparently he collapsed and died in the showers after a friendly game against a team called Montréjeau. He was only 35 years old.

Back to the present, and on a happier note, the club's facilities are awesome. Club president, Pierre-Yves Revol, has invested a lot of money in the club, which includes a purpose-built training facility. There is a large gymnasium, two changing sheds, a treatment room, plunge pool, offices and two training pitches.

L'entraînment. Training. At my first training I learn that you are expected to shake everyone's hand — and I mean everyone's! People stop training to shake someone's hand. It's out there. I will discover that every day is the same and that no matter what, you shake hands with everyone and say hello, and only then do you get down to business.

To France

Our Mondays look something like this: We have a gym session where the guys appear to spend more time talking than doing anything else. They do six or seven sets per exercise and there are approximately three exercises to complete. These can take anywhere from an hour to an hour and a half. Back home we'd be in and out in 45 minutes having done eight exercises plus abdominals.

After weights we do speed work, or, for those who have played, there is a slow run. It means trainings last for between two and two and a half hours. After training we go and eat *déjeuner* (lunch). This is the biggest meal of the day for the French and they like to take anything from two to two and a half hours for their *siesta*. The entire town comes to a standstill; nothing is open and won't be until three-ish. I say 'ish' because they may open sooner, or perhaps later, and in fact they might not reopen at all. It's their prerogative so too bad if it's a matter of urgency — to you! So, we sit and eat. Come 4 pm we have training again, basically skills and defence, and by about 6 pm our day is over.

On Tuesday I get my first taste of scrummaging à la French style. The day begins with a power weights session that runs for an hour and then we go straight into forward drills followed by scrummaging. The first part of the rugby skills session is standard — mauling, plays off the maul and cleaning out mauls. They don't have rucks here. Apparently, the crowd go mental, and the opposition get riled too if you are seen to be spitting someone out the back of a ruck and that's why everything is a maul.

When it comes to scrummaging the club has a massive scrum machine with hydraulics, brakes and gauges all over it. It looks like some kind of bizarre steam engine, quite different from what we use in New Zealand where our scrum machines are more likely to be made of wood and padded bags and bear a resemblance to a sled.

But it's not just the machines that are poles apart. The French also scrum differently to New Zealanders. They are much higher set and the binds are all different. At home it's the props who set off the hooker. Over here the hooker wants you to set on him. The locks and flankers all crotch grip, whereas in New Zealand the flankers don't bind on to the prop. In my first scrum I feel like I'm riding a horse while having a fight with a train. But after a few hits I start to get the hang of this contraption and also of what my fellow team members want from me. After the second scrum, it feels pretty comfortable, not quite so foreign, and I'm confident I can get used to French ways.

I also find out that I'm going to be playing on Saturday. It's an away game at Clermont Ferrand. Christophe Urios, the forwards' coach, and Philippe Berot, the backs' coach, are a little concerned about jet lag. But I tell them that with the ABs we are expected to travel and play a test match within the same short turnaround and assure them I'll be okay to play.

We have a double training session on Wednesday — attack in the morning and defence in the afternoon. These trainings are similar to back home and involve full contact and opposed training with the B team, because tomorrow, Thursday, is our day off.

Excusez-moi de vous déranger. Sorry to bother you. I might be full of running out on the training pitch but I'm practically running on empty when it comes to gas. Not the rear-end kind you may be thinking of, not even as 'in a blast', but *gazole*, meaning diesel. After training I ask one of the boys where the nearest gas station is. He directs me to the depot just down the road from our training ground. Unfortunately, I don't think to ask him how to put gas in the car. Why would I? How hard could it be for goodness' sake? I've been filling up a car ever since I learned to drive! But, of course, I wasn't in France then.

On pulling up to the pumps, I get out of the car and stare at this machine. All the instructions are in French. I have no idea how it works. I punch some buttons and squeeze the bejaysus out of the nozzle. Nothing happens. I decide to drive into the next lane where you can use your bankcard. Bad idea as it turns out. The depot is one of the biggest and busiest in Castres and I quickly have a queue of locals, two cars thick, up my bumper. In my shocking French I ask the lady parked behind me if she can show me how to use the machine. She looks at me in horror and retreats into her car. Feeling useless, I hop back into mine and try to drive off, only to realise you have to pay at the booth and the barrier arm to exit the place is down. Sigh. More pidgin French needed. I battle my way through to the lady in the booth and try to explain that I have no gas and I don't know how to use the machine. Can she help me? She stays mute, glaring at me like a number of the motorists have done. Whether she feels sorry for me or is just plain insulted, I'll never know. She raises the barrier arm and sends me on my way.

I hatch a Plan B. I'll drive home via the back road and save my search for gazole until another day. I take the route driven on my first trip into Castres, and using my Maori instinct think I'll be just fine. However, 30 minutes later (it takes about 10- to- 15 minutes to circumnavigate Castres) I find myself on my way to another town, Mazamet. Out on the open road I realise my mistake so decide to make a U-turn back to town. Lights flash at me from both directions, I am copping abuse (justified unfortunately) from the locals, but I follow the signposts back to Castres, arriving from the opposite side of town. I guess my Maori instinct is a little jet-lagged.

But I find a gas station where you can fill your tank with less rigmarole than the last one. Excited and comforted by the familiarity this system offers, I start to fill the tank. Nothing. My New Zealand bankcard doesn't seem to be working. Thinking I've done everything right I notice a sign in a really obscure place on the pump — only French bankcards accepted here. With the light shining brightly to indicate my tank is almost empty but having no French bankcards or accounts, there is nothing I can do but crawl back to my hotel and be grateful that Castres is only a small town. My Maori instinct is definitely jet-lagged.

Thursday is my day off and, unsurprisingly, first up on my agenda is GAS. I drive to training and do a cardio workout, cycling for 30 minutes and thinking I could be in need of a bike fulltime if I don't get the car filled up soon. After my workout I'm back on my mission and think it will finally be accomplished when I find a petrol station near the training ground. This one has an attendant. It's a straightforward transaction, pay at the counter-type place. I put the nozzle in my car. Nothing. Again. The attendant comes out and informs me that they're out of *gazole*. Meanwhile, my car light continues to register that I'm running on almost empty.

I'm going to have to go back to one of the stations I'd last visited. I take what I hope is the quickest route and, would you believe it, I strike a parade! It's a celebration to commemorate the end of the German occupation of France, post Second World War. The police have blocked off the main road and are detouring traffic through back streets. I have no choice but to go with the flow. Eventually it occurs to me that nothing is familiar and I'm lost. With the car

To France

practically hopping, I round a corner and — lo and behold — good ol' instinct is back again, there's a gas station. Rolling in, the attendant comes out to tend to the car. No more pidgin French needed. I hand her 20 euros and watch to see how they operate the pumps. Because I'm lost, I point in the direction I was travelling and utter the word 'Castres'. She shakes her head, does an about turn and points. Ah, *that* way. Okay, I may have been going the wrong way but in the end it's turned out all right.

4
Game On

Le jeu. The game. Saturday, 13 November is match day and I have to be at the airport by 8.15 am for what is to be an evening game. I find the club's travel protocol quite amusing. If we win a game, we get to fly to the next one if it is any great travelling distance away. If we lose, we take a bus. Fortunately, because of the big win against Biarritz a week prior, we are treated to a flight instead of a six-hour bus trip.

We arrive in Clermont-Ferrand, situated west of Lyon in the Auvergne region, and spend the day at our hotel prior to the match against Montferrand, scheduled for 7 pm. My preparation for the match hasn't changed from the way I'd prepare for a game in New Zealand. However, the French method of getting ready is vastly different to what I'm used to. They sit in the foyer playing poker — for cash — and quaff unbelievable amounts of coffee, cup after cup after cup, and there's plenty of talk of the general banter type and I find it hard to imagine they're actually preparing to play a game tonight.

The pre-match meals are 100 per cent French, with no concessions made for the modern-day professional athlete. We begin with salads and bread, followed by meat, pasta and mashed potatoes. They frown upon us eating between meals so my protein shakes have to be taken discreetly.

The standard formulae for most coach's meetings prior to the game are universal. However, having them conducted in French is not. I have a strategy worked out. I sit on one side of the captain of our team, Mario Ledesma, an Argentinean who speaks French and English, and another English speaking team-mate sits on the other. Mario listens to the coach and then relays the information to us. I find the process amusing because our coach talks for an age and then Mario says, 'Ah, don't worry about that part' or imparts something simple such as, 'You need to hit mauls'.

I've come to realise that if the French can be considered passionate about their rugby, they are just as passionate about their language. They often take a long time to explain something that native English speakers would sum up in a matter of a few words. Hence the coach's long speeches. They are full of emotion and most of the time that's the point he is putting across — his emotion. In between all the florid phrases and gesticulations are his instructions for the game. Slowly, we get drip fed the message. It reminds me of Chinese whispers, all of us sitting in a row and passing on what's being said. I'm tempted to be really cheeky one day and pass on a random message just to see what happens.

We arrive at the stadium two hours prior to the match. This seems a long time to be getting ready. Most of the guys go out on to the field, converse and joke around with the opposition. I cannot comprehend this because during the game they end up in fights, punching each other, getting sent off, and then they are back to hugging each other as they walk off the field. Crazy Frenchmen.

I start on the bench for my first game for Castres because the coaches are still worried about possible jet lag. The first half is a 'shit fight' — no words can sum it up better — an amateur boxing match with two guys sent off within eight minutes, two more are yellow-carded and yet there are still 20 minutes remaining in the first half. My initial thought is: 'What have I got myself into?'

Les Blacks. The All Blacks. Right at this moment my new rugby career seems light years away from my days as an All Black. My memory of the moment I found out I'd made the All Blacks is as clear as if it happened yesterday. In fact it was just over six years ago in late August 1998. I was living in Dunedin, playing for Otago and the Highlanders, and on that particular winter's day I'd decided to go pig hunting with a few mates. We went out early, about 5 am, and at 11 o'clock we decided to call it quits and head back home. The radio was on but I wasn't listening, I was just sitting there, looking out the window and minding my own business. Suddenly I get a slap on my head and Brian Steel, not yet my father-in-law, was saying, 'Congratulations, you've made the All Blacks.'

I didn't take him seriously. In fact I borrowed some of my father's words and told Brian to 'get ****** and stop bullshitting me'. I had good reason. He used to ring me up and pretend to be John Hart, ask me how I was going and I'd be on the other end of the phone, all prim and proper until he'd burst out with, 'You bloody blouse, it's me!'

Le Rugbyman

It took him quite a while to convince me that this time he wasn't pulling my leg and we changed the channels on the radio until I heard the news myself. But it didn't really sink in until I got home and on my landline there were about 10 messages from people wanting to get hold of me, and one of those was from the real John Hart. I rang and he confirmed that, yes, I was selected in the squad for the game against Australia. They weren't sure what the story was with Olo Brown's injury but I'd been called into the team as cover. It was midweek when I heard that Olo wasn't going to recover in time and I got the nod to play. I was absolutely stoked.

Funnily enough, I didn't really feel I was with the All Blacks, even when I joined the squad prior to flying out to Australia and despite learning the moves and training alongside them. I think that was because so many of the guys were familiar to me; they were people I played with or against all the time. Two of my Otago mates, Carl Hoeft and Anton Oliver, had made the side earlier in the season.

It took being presented with my All Black jersey to make it all real. It was at that moment I felt *hey, this isn't a dream, this is actually happening*. Manager Mike Banks presented me with my jersey and that's when I realised I was going to play a test.

I was rooming with Josh Kronfeld whom I'd known for ages. I'm sure they put him with me just to keep me calm. Josh is a pretty relaxed kind of guy but even his laid-back influence couldn't stop me from feeling really, really nervous before the game and when I was going through the time-honoured spluttering, dry-retching routine.

And then we were running out onto the pitch at the Sydney Football Stadium. It's hard to explain the feeling. Part of it was like I was in a dream. I was trying to absorb everything, the environment around me, and also trying desperately not to let my nerves get the better of me. I didn't want to start vomiting out on the field so I kept telling myself to calm down, don't throw up. But once the haka kicked in, wow, it was all on.

Looking back, the game passed in a blur and there's not that much I remember about the actual match other than the haka and then being absolutely gutted that I'd lost my first test. The final score was 14–19 to Australia. But I do remember Anton Oliver presenting me with my test tie and the profound words he spoke to me that day are the words I've tried to live by in my rugby life. I've also tried to instil their essence in younger players I've had an opportunity to influence. What Anton said to me will remain private but his words were to do with the tradition of the black jersey and the mana associated with being an All Black.

Les mémoires. Memories. Looking back, being an All Black has presented me with so many memorable moments. One of the greatest was meeting Nelson Mandela before what turned out to be my last test match, against South Africa at Johannesburg, and getting to shake the great man's hand. Nelson Mandela epitomises togetherness. To me, he's an awesome man, because of what he stands for, the things he's been through, and being able to forgive people for that. I've also met Sir Edmund Hillary and that was another huge honour. He came down to the Waikato to speak to the All Blacks in 2003. I asked him to sign a $5 bill and I've put it away for my kids. Just being in the presence of people such as Mandela and Sir Edmund, people who've done great things, is very humbling. If it wasn't for rugby I probably would never have met them.

I've also met the Queen. We went to Buckingham Palace in 2002. I have a photograph of me with Queen Elizabeth and that picture is among our treasured belongings that will be coming to France. Meeting royalty is an awesome experience because I think that most of us, at some stage in our lives, have dreamed of meeting a king, a queen, or a princess.

On the field, equalling and then setting a new world record for tries scored by a prop is top of my list of magic moments. I scored my eighth, the record-equalling try, in 2003 when we beat Canada 68–8 during the World Cup pool match in Melbourne. I had to work hard for it too. The All Blacks scored 10 tries during that game and Mils Muliaina, playing on the right wing, nabbed four of them. I broke the record a week later when we played Tonga in Brisbane. It was a huge win for us, 91–7, and the All Blacks scored 13 tries. Mine came early in the second half, in the 46th minute to be precise, and I thoroughly enjoyed the moment.

Most of my tries have come from rucks or close to the line but I'd like it recorded that I had to work hard for a few of them too! I was also denied a few as well because there were times when too many people arrived to pile on top of me and obscure the ref's view. I got my tenth international try in July 2004 when the All Blacks beat the Pacific Islands team 41–26.

Do I have a favourite match? On a personal level it would have to be the game against Wales played at Hamilton in June 2003. We won that game 55–3 and, yes, I did score a try. Also, I think it was the most complete game I ever played for the All Blacks. Everything went right that day: I was dominant at scrum time, I had presence around the field, I was running with the ball in hand, off-loading well, and I went over the line three times. The ref awarded me only one try and I guess I have to be content with that. There was one clear-cut opportunity to get another during the game but I decided to help out a mate who'd played 30-odd tests and had yet to score a try. I thought I'd pop the ball to him and what happend? He dropped it!

Another memorable match and for very different reasons was the first test against England in 2004. What made it special for me was the way the boys handled it. We'd had a week together prior to the game and I thought we did an excellent job in the way we came together and were able to put the horrors of the World Cup campaign behind us. And then to play the way we did, beating England comprehensively 36–3! It was my first big test as a loosehead too. I was marking Julian White, who was quite highly rated, and I think I came out on top in that contest.

Sur la touche. On the sideline. Of course for all the highs rugby gives me, there are lows as well. My worst moments are off-the-field ones and seem to mostly involve coaches, especially during my earlier All Black years. I was 24 years old when I first made the All Blacks and I'd come in to replace Olo Brown, the best tighthead in the world at that time. I believe I was expected to pick up at the same level as Olo, in fact be better than he was, and I don't think the coaches took into consideration that I was coming to them with no test experience. It seemed to me that they wanted a quick-fix solution to their propping problems.

When I got the call-up to the All Blacks I went in thinking I'd earned my spot. But was I as good as Olo back then? Of course not. But seven seasons on and having played against the world's best, yes, I'd rate myself on a par with Olo and I hope we will both be remembered as top-class players. I don't think you can compare players of one era with another, as the game is constantly changing, evolving. Today's game is faster than ever, the rules are different and the job description of each position has changed — especially for props. Props are expected to be able to run with the ball in hand and the whole concept of being nothing more than a thick concrete mixer no longer exists.

Being a front-row forward is no excuse for leaving the brain in a bag by the changing room door and collecting it after a game. Rugby is a thinking game and props, just like the rest of their teammates, are expected to use their grey matter.

La déception. Disappointment. There are times, though, when coaches could use their noggins a bit more as well. One major disappointment during my time as an All Black was being rapped over the knuckles in front of the whole team before the first game of the '99 World Cup. John Hart and Peter Sloane went around the team and gave a pep talk to each player. I can recall my mates Carl Hoeft and Anton Oliver receiving positive comments and even some helpful advice and then suddenly, when John got to me, he switched tack, boomed 'and *you*' and went into a spiel about how I believed in my own hype. I was stunned.

At the time adidas had just come on board as the major sponsor of the All Blacks. For whatever reason, they decided I was a marketable commodity and had used me for their campaign. My image was plastered over every poster, booklet and aeroplane imaginable, something I'd never asked for. It's a part of being a professional rugby player that you have no control over and once you become an All Black the union effectively owns your name — your identity, come to that.

And here was the All Black coach telling me that *I thought* I was some kind of superstar, a tag that in his opinion wasn't warranted. He went on to tell me that I was the sole reason for the team losing the Bledisloe test that year — a statement I find offensive as well as ironic. I'd been under the impression that, along with the other 14 players on my team that day, we were all playing hard to win.

John then attacked the way I did the haka, saying I was a 'show pony' because I didn't do what everyone else was doing. I was insulted. I'm Maori, it's part of my culture, and I'd been in the Kapa Haka team at school. Bottom line: the haka is just as important to me as the actual game. And the thought I put into it, the way I do it, is how I show what being an All Black means to me, and how I demonstrate my respect for all the All Blacks who have gone before me. In my opinion the haka should be done properly and players should give it their all. The pukana (eye bulging) and whetero (poking out the tongue) I give at the end of the haka represents my individuality but it is also a personal challenge to my opposition.

I heard later that the reason I'd been singled out for such attention was because a 'peer' (who shall remain nameless) from Otago told the coaching staff to piss me off prior to the match in order to fire me up and make me play better.

Nothing could be further from the truth. Sure, the verbal attack made me angry and a lot more antsy going in to what was then — and still is — the biggest rugby competition in the world. But making me angry isn't the way to make me play well. It never has been. I'm the type of person who plays a lot better if I am calm and focused in my build-up to a match. I'm disappointed that John, with his supposed man-management skills, hadn't worked that out for himself. I was so disturbed by what was said that I wrote about it in the journal I had been keeping during that tournament.

It probably wasn't until I moved back to Auckland in 2002 that I realised if I was going to play at my best I'd have to switch off to what some coaches were saying, and once I did that I started playing some really good rugby. My game has definitely benefited from that approach because I've been able to concentrate on what I want to achieve rather than worry about what I think the coach is thinking of me, or whether I'm likely to be there for the next game because he likes or dislikes me. It's just one of those things, part and parcel of rugby; you get your good coaches and your not-so-good ones and it's important not to let them rile you.

There's no doubt that being a pro sportsman means you work in a pretty fickle environment. Sure, you have a contract but it's still a match-to-match, week-to-week sort of job. These days, you have one bad game and, if the management is confident you can fix the problems, you'll get another opportunity. But for a long time I didn't think that was the case in New Zealand. There were the superstars who never got dropped and then there were the guys who were brought in, seemingly to just fill the void until the next superstar came along. I've seen it with a lot of players, not just myself — I was quite fortunate to be there fairly consistently for seven seasons although I had my share of being in and then out of the side. But I saw some guys coming in one season, playing all right but not outstandingly, and then they were gone the next.

Rugby is a team sport but it's also about individuals. You might be doing your job at scrum time but someone else isn't doing theirs and it impacts on everyone else. Most of the time you actually end up looking better because you're doing the job of two players but a lot of outside people don't see that.

But that's rugby. I never got nasty or snarky about it, I just carried on and tried to think things through — *How can I fix this?* or *What can I do to improve my game?*

Game On

There are all the clichés about front rows and dumb props. I hope I've gone some way to help disprove that old chestnut. I don't believe you can play at the top level of rugby without having a reasonable level of intelligence. Rugby provides mental as well as physical challenges. It's a-game-once-a-week-at-least existence and no matter what competition you're in, Super 12, NPC or the All Blacks, there are no easy matches. Every time you take the field it's an important game and you've got to be up for it. It's tough — week in, week out — and the ones who can handle it mentally are the ones who last, who make the All Blacks and are there consistently when it comes to team selection.

It helps if you have a strong support crew. It's not easy for them; they hear first hand what people are saying out on the street and are probably reading more of the papers than you are. Not many people are likely to walk up to a player and tell him he's had a shit game but they are more than happy to pass their opinion on to your brother or your sister. It means your family has to become as mentally tough as you are.

But the good times far outweigh the bad and there's no other job I would rather have done. I loved being an All Black and I think I've grown as a person because of my experiences with the team.

And it's thanks to my time with the All Blacks that I'm now in France, sitting on the sideline and at the moment watching two teams trying to beat each other into submission. Referees here aren't as pedantic as they are back home and they seem to let a lot slip by the wayside. I've heard that refs in France can be shocking, and it is quite common for them to cave in to the pressure from the home-team supporters. Apparently, when you play an away game you're likely to be 10 points behind before the game even starts.

Le Rugbyman

Les actes sont plus éloquents que les paroles. Actions speak louder than words. Halftime arrives and I get the nod to go on. I'm really keen to get my hands on the ball. Within a matter of minutes I get my wish, take the ball and make a short break before offloading. I'm into the game.

But my first scrum is a shocker! We have seven forwards to their eight and we stack up the far side of the scrum — not my side. However, the opposition stacks up my side and I end up walking backwards a couple of metres. But we score. The mind boggles!

Our number eight picked up the ball, saw the opposition were concentrating on smashing me and he ran like the wind for 15 metres, past their flanker who was still pushing against me — head down, bum up — to score the try. It looked like a planned move!

The rest of the game goes well and there are no more problems with the scrums. Ten minutes into the half I am initiated into French rugby, courtesy of having my first scrap. There's a bit of argy-bargy after a scrum so I decide to let some fly. It must look quite comical because I'm throwing my arms around, trying to connect with anyone within reach. I won't be surprised if I get a yellow card but, lo and behold, it's our lock who is sidelined for 10 minutes. And he didn't do anything. Perhaps that's his punishment for not being emotional enough about the game?

The rest of the game is pretty smooth going, much like a massive game of scrag. Both teams take the lead at various times until, finally, two points down and two minutes into injury time our first-five dropkicks the winning goal. It's an important win for us because Montferrand are a class team who, despite being near the bottom of the table, put out a good side against us.

I'm happy with my game and feel as though I've earned my first stripes.

5

Spooked

Ma famille et le fantôme. My family and the ghost. Tuesday 16 November is a red-letter day because Juanita and the girls are arriving. I've really missed them and 11.15 am can't come quick enough. However, there is a training session to get through first after which the coaches throw in an impromptu meeting. I'm running an hour behind schedule by the time I get to the airport at Toulouse but fortunately the flight is delayed and our arrivals synchronise perfectly.

But I'm not alone to greet my family; the press turn up wanting pictures of our reunion. Although Juanita's sister Rebecca has accompanied her on the trip over to help with the girls, the Singapore-Toulouse leg was a tough one for my whanau. Juanita is horrified at the idea of having her post-voyage photo splashed across the newspapers, but the girls, exhausted but excited to see their daddy, pose with me for the cameras, which satisfies the snappers.

Le Rugbyman

I am eager to show them what I hope will become our new 'house'. It's only a temporary measure; we can rent it for a month so we don't have to stay in a hotel and until we find something suitable for a family of four.

I'm confident this initial place will take Juanita's breath away. It's in the grounds of a chateau and although our house might be part of a stable block, it is by no means a humble abode. Rather, it's an impressive three-storey, six-bedroom residence that is around 400 years old.

Rumour has it that the chateau's original owners were French royalty — maybe that's why, as mere Kiwi plebs, we've been offered the stable-house accommodation! The setting is stunning — sprawling fields, a lake and walking tracks, roads from a long-ago lifetime crisscrossing the estate. There is a huge shrine featuring the Virgin Mary and a bell tower at a crossroads, stone-carved seats and tables and wrought-iron crosses. Water on the property continues to be drawn from the many wells that are dotted across the grounds.

The chateau is a beautiful building, an imposing five or six storeys if you include the attic and basement levels. By examining the positioning of the windows you can work out where grand rooms such as ballrooms are situated, and the outlines of sweeping staircases and grand foyers are clearly visible.

Outside the servants' entrance and near the scullery, which is partially underground, is the bell that tradesmen must have rung when delivering supplies for the household. Shutters flank each window frame — to us it looks more French than French.

The estate contains two large stables that must have housed a score of horses in their day. At the end of each stableyard is a house, ours being one of them, and there is also a woodshed, swimming pool, pool house and garage space. It looks perfect.

Spooked

We almost have to pinch ourselves. Here we are, the Meeuws family from New Zealand, used to newly built homes with all their mod cons, getting the opportunity to spend time living in the shadow of a wonderful and historic chateau on the other side of the world. It's so far removed from anything we've ever lived in before and seems a fabulous way to kick off our French adventure. It could be like living a dream.

In fact, it's a nightmare.

Looking back, the warning signs were there all along. Initially, I went to view the house with fellow Kiwi and Castres team-mate, Brad Fleming. A real estate agent took us on a tour of the place and all was fine until we reached the third level and I walked into the room closest to the stairwell. As soon as I crossed the threshold all the hairs on the back of my neck stood on end. I felt a chill run through me. Was I the only one to feel disturbed? I turned to Brad and whispered, 'Did you feel that?' He nodded in agreement.

I backtracked out of the room and went downstairs. Nothing else about the place bothered me and I brushed aside what had happened up in that third-floor room. I mean, what really had occurred up there? I'd felt something strange but it was nothing tangible — just a feeling. Maybe I was still suffering from jet lag and letting my imagination get the better of me — and of Brad. But I decided not to make a firm decision about the place until Juanita looked it over.

It's a beautiful late-autumn day when we all return to the house, which, in the sunlight, looks stunning. Our daughters, still exhausted from the arduous flight, are asleep in the car and we decide to leave them there while we tour the property. Juanita and I wander through the rooms, floor by floor. Eventually we reach the top storey and I watch my wife enter the room nearest to the stairwell. She steps in and then steps straight back out. I ask her the same question I'd put to Brad. 'Did you feel that?'

When she says yes, I'm pleased. It's a relief and I think, 'Cool, I'm not the only one who feels like that.' Anyway, after some discussion Juanita and I decide to take the place. It's hard not to be enchanted by its size and spectacular location and there is another factor — we don't want to appear rude to those who've gone to all the trouble of finding it for us.

We climb back into the car, spend the rest of the day organising our belongings and making a much-needed trip to the supermarket, and by the time we are ready to return to the house it is evening. Darkness has fallen.

As we approach the house, Eva, now wide awake and raring to go, starts getting all excited.

'Is this our new house?' she keeps repeating as we pull up, her eyes almost out on stalks as she tries to take in all that she can see. Our new address makes a pretty impressive sight in the gathering gloom and it certainly dwarfs any bouncy castle that Eva's ever seen. No house we've lived in or visited back in New Zealand comes close to the grandeur of this place. I park close to the door, get out of the car and go and unlock the house before I fetch Eva. The girl is wired by this stage!

'Dad, Dad, where's the little girl?' she asks.

'Who?' I say, having no idea what she is burbling about.

'*Viens*. The little girl. This is the little girl's house.'

I don't understand what or whom she is talking about. 'What do you mean?' I ask her as we go inside. It seems as though she is talking French and rubbish all at the same time.

Spooked

'There's a little girl here.'

I think, 'Oh yeah,' and say to her, 'Whereabouts?'

She says, 'She's up there.'

I still don't get it so we go back outside and she points up to the window of the room on the third floor. I am like, 'Okay then,' not quite sure what is going on here.

Even when we we're back inside and starting to unpack our things, Eva won't let the subject drop. She keeps asking me where the little girl is. I ask her if she wants to go and have a look and we make our way up to the third floor.

There's no one there. No one is waiting to greet us in the room at the top of the stairs. Eva is confused. She can't understand why 'the little girl' isn't waiting to play.

The following evening I decide to rearrange some of the furniture. I take the bed bases out of our room, which is on the second level, and shift them into the stairwell. On our floor, it's a poorly lit space, but higher up, on the third floor, the light is shining. As I'm moving the bed bases I suddenly go cold. My eyes are drawn upwards. A shadow moves across the wall and into the third floor bedroom. I leave the bed bases and bolt back into our room trying to appear calm. I don't make any comment about what's happened because I don't want to scare Juanita.

But it's not a happy house. It feels like someone is watching us — constantly. The girls are restless. One night Juanita thinks she hears one of them whispering 'Mummy, Mummy' in her ear. But when she checks they are, thankfully, asleep. But they are uneasy, they need constant reassurance that we are there for them and one day they're too scared to leave their beds and they scream and scream.

Little things start happening. Shutters which close over the windows, held in place by levers which you must twist to undo, are suddenly wide open. Ash from a fireplace is strewn over our things. After one particularly restless night, I open up our bedroom shutters, making quite a racket in the process, to find a flock of up to 50 black crows sitting on the ground outside. Despite the noise they remain motionless.

It's like living on the set of a Hollywood blockbuster, *Scary Movie* and all its sequels rolled into one . . . are the Meeuws family mere extras or the unwitting stars of the show, playing out a script but ignorant as to where and when the plot is revealed? Can we expect to see an ethereal Nicole Kidman floating down the stairs? Will headless horsemen come trotting through the foyer? How long before our daughter tells us, 'I see dead people'? Who is directing this show?

Juanita feels she has to keep busy the whole time she is in the house. She also confesses that the macabre thought 'the dead have come to greet us' flashed through her mind as we'd first driven up to the house. Now she tells me!

Talking over the situation at the breakfast table one day, she and Rebecca arrive at a seemingly illogical conclusion: Eva's imaginary 'playmate' is about eight or nine years old. It's just a gut feeling they have, and can't shake off. Common sense, something that is becoming increasingly hard to find within these walls, would suggest there is no earthly reason to back up their conviction. They try to blame these notions on jet lag. We all do. How long can the effects of jet lag last? It has to be a more reasonable explanation than the one we don't want to make. We don't believe in ghosts. Can I say that with feeling?

Rebecca leaves and we are truly on our own. Or are we? The last straw comes when I am at training one morning. Juanita is in the kitchen with the girls, giving them their breakfast. All the doors in the house are shut, mainly to help keep the heat in. Suddenly she hears a door open, creaking the way old doors are inclined to do, and then it slams shut. She sticks her head out into the hallway but there's no one around. She goes back to tending the kids when she hears a thudding noise that sounds as if someone is walking up the stairs. She grabs the kids, bundles them into the car and drives away, and she doesn't return until she's sure I'll be back from training.

We decide to spend the rest of the day away from the house and we lunch with some people from the team and do a few errands. We try to find alternative accommodation and for the short-term we can crash at Brad's place. But that is still a fortnight away. It is with a degree of trepidation that we return to the stable-house. The window in the main lounge appears to have blown open despite the shutters being closed. There's no way this window could have opened by itself — it's got a massive lock on it.

Somehow we make it through the remaining days. Fortunately, we don't have much to pack and on the day we move out it doesn't take us long to get our belongings together. As we drive away Eva pipes up, 'This house makes me very sick.'

We're reluctant to talk about events at the stable house. We don't want to offend the locals and we certainly don't want them to think we're the kind of people who might decide that living in a foreign country equates with having paranormal experiences. Of course we have imaginations, but we don't believe they are overactive.

However, we find reassurance close at hand. The stable-house has been rented out previously and to one of my team-mates, captain Mario Ledesma who plays hooker, *le talonneur*. Like us, his stay was eventful — and short. We swap experiences. He tells me about the pentagram that appeared in the misted-up bathroom mirror every time he had a shower. It was never in the same place twice but always there. It's enough to send more shivers up the spine. The pentagram is a well-known symbol of the occult world.

His experiences with doors and windows seemingly blowing open by themselves are similar to ours. He tells me how the side doors leading out to the garden blew open one night — this despite the fact they were latched with not just one but three locks. He wasn't alone at feeling uneasy in the house. His wife, mother-in-law and mother were all frightened, and on one occasion all three were overcome by a feeling of foreboding at exactly the same moment and despite being in different parts of the house.

As expected, the real estate agent we've been dealing with is sceptical about our reasons for moving out. It's difficult for us to admit that we think the house is haunted. We try to convince her we're not mad, and that strange and unsettling things actually happened. She makes some inquiries. It turns out that the chateau was indeed built by a family with connections to royalty and it was a place that saw much death, especially during the French Revolution. According to an elderly farmer who lives in the area, he remembers that the last person to die on the estate was a little girl. He reckons she was eight or nine years old.

We mull over the findings. What did Eva mean when she used the word '*viens*' in association with seeing the child at the window? The French verb *venir* means 'to come'. Could Eva have seen someone beckoning her? We don't know and we certainly won't ask our daughter. Apart from telling us that the little girl is 'over at the big house', she doesn't talk about who or what she saw that first evening.

Spooked

But our stay at the stable-house has definitely affected our daughter. Eva is not her usual happy self. We now have to leave the light on at night for her and she requires constant reassurance. We can only hope that whatever unsettling memories she has of our time in the stable-house will quickly fade.

Le camping. Camping. We've kicked Brad out of his apartment and taken over his one-bedroom flat until we can find another place to rent. Fortunately, his wife's in New Zealand at the moment so the accommodation shuffle displaces only one person. Brad has moved in with a team-mate.

Renting à la French style proves to be yet another weird experience. They sure do things a hell of a lot differently to New Zealand but I guess that's what moving to a foreign country is all about. What seems absurd to us is commonplace to them.

Rental properties ain't what we are used to. We see houses that are furnished with items such as a sofa, beds, dishwasher, perhaps a fridge, clothes drier, maybe a table and chairs or sheets and blankets. But the oven is missing. There are no guarantees a house will come complete with what we would consider the basics, such as light fittings or, hang on, what about kitchen cupboards! Because we're looking to rent we don't want to have to invest in the outfitting of a kitchen — it's an expense we haven't budgeted for and when we eventually move on we aren't planning to literally take the kitchen sink with us!

The good news is we eventually find a place. It's a 15-minute walk from the town centre and has a huge back garden. The house is relatively modern; well, it's 20 years old, but that seems positively up-to-the-minute after our spell in the centuries-old haunted house. The décor may take some getting used to — there is wallpaper everywhere, awfully garish prints and colours, and here's a new one, even the doors are wallpapered! Of course open plan is a concept that hadn't reached the French 20 years ago — it's not the big go now either come to that — but there are lots of bedrooms and the kitchen is a generous size, especially when compared to other houses we have viewed. Best news of all, it is a workable kitchen complete with cupboards, fridge, a dishwasher and an oven and hob. We find it quite strange that most of the houses we have looked through, either when we've been searching for somewhere to live or been out visiting, have small kitchens. It seems odd considering the importance that food and its preparation have in the daily lives of the French people.

The layout of the house seems somewhat bizarre — the toilets are in pokey hideaway corners, almost as if they didn't want to include such items when designing the place. But we think it will be perfect for us. The only thing we've had to invest in is a washing machine and we decide to buy new bed linen and curtains.

The bad news is we can't move in until mid-December. It means we will have to continue living out of suitcases for another couple of weeks and we're going to have to decamp to the house of another team-mate for a few days during that time because Brad's wife is due back.

L'essence du vie. Fuel of life. But life goes on. I still have to play rugby and as a family we need fuel for our internal engines. A trip to the supermarket becomes top priority. It quickly becomes evident how much I am going to rely on Juanita. I can't read a word of French and I've no idea where to look for things or what the labels mean. But I enjoy wandering up and down the aisles. French supermarkets are a foodie's heaven. Okay, as expected they are a little short on items that you may use for certain Polynesian, Asian or Pakeha dishes but there is an abundance of other goods. You may find three aisles dedicated to chocolate and lollies and an alcohol section that takes up four aisles — fantastic wines from all over France and dirt cheap to boot. No complaints here! There's an entire aisle devoted to various bottled waters and two aisles for biscuits, breakfast breads and pre-packaged cakes.

Fresh food is in abundance, along with cheeses, conventional meats such as poultry and beef and cured meats (the Dutch part of me loves this section of the supermarket). There are two aisles given over to cleaning products and an amazing five aisles dedicated to personal grooming products. I'm astounded. Just the other day, while reading *Lonely Planet France*, I came across an interesting statistic: only 47 per cent of French people bathe or shower every day and soap consumption in France is half that of the United Kingdom's. Apparently the French use less deodorants than any other country in Europe but every man, woman and child spends, on average, the equivalent of $100 a year on beauty products.

Our problems are not about products that clean or pamper the body. Both Eva and I suffer from allergies and in Eva's case she cannot eat nuts or eggs. We soon discover that most things here seem to be made with some form of egg or contain nuts. Fortunately, Allergy New Zealand has sent us some information to assist us in translating the French to English on various products and that helps us greatly. Slowly, we are working out which products are safe.

Our biggest challenge to date is dining out. As we get better at translating and understanding the menus we will hopefully become adept at working out which dishes are safe for Eva and me to eat.

Le Rugbyman

The challenges of living in a foreign-speaking country continue to be many and varied.

Entre équipes voisines. The local derby. Today we play Toulouse, a club that offered me a contract earlier in the year only to renege at the eleventh hour. Thus, I have a point to prove — a motivating factor just in case I need one. I'm anticipating your basic hell-for-leather big brother versus little brother all-out slugfest.

Because our previous game resulted in victory we are treated to some amazing accommodation in Soreze for the build-up to our match, which will be a home game. The village is located at the foot of the Black Mountain and it is a magnificent example of medieval architecture, some of the houses dating back to the 16th and 17th centuries. I know my thoughts are supposed to be solely about the game later today, but as I look around it is easy to imagine the Musketeers on horseback, trotting through the narrow but pretty streets.

Période d'échauffement. The warm-up. Back to the present, I make an effort to prepare myself for the pre-match drills — so different to anything I've ever experienced. In New Zealand, the boys get together, the backs doing their thing while the forwards mark out 5 m and 15 m and go through our repertoire of lineouts. It's all over in 15 to 20 minutes.

To my horror — and I mean horror — in France that 15–20 minutes is taken up with a warm-up that involves a lot of running up and down on the spot while counting to 10 in French, hands waving in the air, heads bobbing up and down. It's like taking part in a 1980s aerobics class. We continue with a lot of squatting on the

Spooked

spot, followed by basic crossover drills, the sort of thing I was doing as a 12 year old.

I have to keep my head down and at times pull my shirt up to my mouth to disguise the fact I'm laughing. At one point I have my shirt over my mouth and one of the boys thinks someone has farted. 'Can you smell something offensive?' he asks. I shake my head and mumble something about being cold.

The warm-up finally completed, it's now time for lineout drills. The problems are more aural than physical, the accents of the halfbacks the thing I have to concentrate on. Learning French is hard for a layman and the problem is compounded by the different dialects among the team. It's another issue I have to grapple with.

We board the bus that will take us back to Castres and to Stade Pierre-Antoine. It is two and a half hours prior to kick-off and we reach our ground with two hours to spare. The trip, although quick, proves an experience. Music blares through the bus, something that would be considered a no-no at home where, if you wanted music you had to bring along your own headphones. I have my usual game face on and wonder how I'm going to occupy the next 45 minutes until I start my usual pre-match routine. I look around. My teammates are either joking around or chatting to our opposition. Ah, different day but same pre-match scenario. Almost.

My pre-match routine has always consisted of me strapping one hour and 15 minutes before the game. This takes quarter of an hour. Then I have a massage to loosen any stiffness in my limbs and when that is done there are 45 minutes until the match begins. I start my personal warm-up and do some stretching before we come together as a team 25 minutes out from kick-off. I have no superstitions, no special undies that I must wear, no lucky charms, no slapping myself or staring into the mirror and trying to intimidate my reflection (unlike someone I know!). All my mental preparation has been dealt with prior to leaving for the game, usually after lineout practice.

But that was then. Now, in France, things are rather different — insanely different in fact. If I thought the lineout warm-up was crazy, I am in for another surprise, a rather nasty one, when we begin our pre-match preparation. In the corridor outside the changing sheds the forwards are huddled together. They start running up and down the hallway, flicking heels to bums, high knees, more squats and hands waving above the head while one of the team screams encouragement at the rest of us. I can only guess at what's being said because it's all in French — at its most excitable.

The eyes of our 'cheerleader' are bulging and it looks as though the veins on his forehead are about to burst. It's like taking part in some weird initiation ritual. The guys start to slap themselves, bashing at their chests and then hitting themselves on the side of the head. I look on in amazement. There is no way I'm going to get into this so I go through the motions without actually making contact with any part of me. A man could injure himself without playing a minute of rugby!

The call for five minutes until kick-off is given and I breathe a huge sigh of relief.

Remembering a story Richard Loe told me, I'm half-expecting the head butting to begin. He said that in a game he played against France, one of the French props walked out onto the field with a blank expression, bruised and with blood pouring from his forehead. Apparently he'd been head-butting the wall in order to psyche himself up before going out to face the All Blacks and almost concussed himself. Perhaps the blank expression indicated that he had.

Spooked

Fortunately, my team-mates resist the temptation to bang their heads against brick walls. We line up, ready to run onto the pitch. I am told to go to the front of the line and lead the team out because the crowd expects it for what is to be my first home game. Sweet. Appreciative of this gesture out I go and the crowd gives me a warm welcome. I'm thrilled and then instantly embarrassed, feel like a prize bullock in fact, because when I turn around I am the lone Castres player on the pitch. My team-mates wait until the applause dies away before joining me.

Unbeknown to me the news that I was to join Castres had created much excitement in this rugby-mad town. Other All Blacks have played for the club: Gary Whetton of course, Frank Bunce and Frano Botica. Another Kiwi, Norm Berryman, has also done a stint here. But that hasn't dulled the townspeople's anticipation for having another of us join their ranks. They are a passionate people who love their rugby and it's a good feeling to know my presence here is regarded in such a positive light.

Le match interminable. The never-ending match. Although I don't know it, I am about to play one of the longest games of my life. There are 15 minutes of injury time played in the first half and the second half will last for an incredible 58 minutes — a total of 33 minutes added on to what will be a pot-boiler of a contest. Toulouse are points up early on but the lead will change hands several times over the course of the match. We are well aware of how important a good result is for our team but three minutes shy of normal fulltime we are still two points down and within striking distance. We pile on the pressure and work our way up to the opposition 22 where we are awarded a penalty, which Richard Dourthe slots to put us ahead 18–17.

Le Rugbyman

The clock indicates fulltime but the referee is obviously enjoying himself so much that he declares eight minutes of injury time remain and that becomes 18. Toulouse regain the lead by virtue of a Jean-Frédéric Dubois dropped goal and with time running out, or so we think, they are hot on attack. Somehow we manage to grapple possession from them and play our way back up field. There is no way through, the Toulouse defence is watertight, but they are powerless to prevent Xavier Sadourny from popping over a dropped goal that puts us back in front by the narrowest of margins at 21–20.

Is it all over now? No way. It turns out there are another 10 minutes to go and Toulouse are peppering our posts with goal attempts. Dubois misses two dropped goal attempts and then it is heart-in-the-mouth stuff as Benoît Baby attempts a penalty shot from 53 m out. His attempt fails and, at long last, the ref blows his whistle for fulltime. The partisan crowd go mental. To beat the big guns from Toulouse is a huge boost and that result moves us to the top of the table of the French championship where, for now, we share first place with two other teams. It takes 20 minutes just to get off the field, to make my way through the deliriously happy throng of Castres supporters. I don't think I've ever shaken so many hands. The celebrations begin in earnest.

I'm exhausted but pleased. I know I played well. But then I get told that one of the match commentators referred to me as a '*beau poulet*'. Translated that comes across as 'chicken' and I'm disappointed, insulted even. Was the commentator trying to suggest I have chicken legs or, worse still, was playing chicken and running away from any involvement in the tough stuff that is part and parcel of a local derby? But I am quickly reassured that *non*, a '*beau poulet*' is a good thing, one of the biggest compliments you can receive in France and I should be honoured by his comment. I might have guessed that anything good in France would be compared to something edible!

Despite the praise, I don't want to get too involved in the post-match hoopla. I have plans for the weekend. Tomorrow the whanau and I are going to visit Carcassonne, an ancient city that dates back two and a half thousand years. It's about an hour's drive from Castres and we are almost giddy with the anticipation of being able to do something touristy in what is the middle of a rugby season.

But my efforts to get home from the club are quickly thwarted. Our own cars are on the other side of town, parked at the club's training facilities from where the bus collected us. I wonder about catching a taxi but apparently they don't run after 7 pm. I have no intention of walking 15 km home having played a game of rugby and so I scout around hoping to find someone who can give me a lift. My team-mates are of no help, most of them have hit the juice. Eventually, after five hours of standing around at the supporters' club, game-sore and tired and chatting to the locals, I find someone to take me home. He's a Tahitian and only too willing to help an Island brother.

It is half-past two in the morning when I am dropped off at home and I am as sober as a judge. As I climb wearily into bed I wonder if having a few beers might have got me home earlier and easier and maybe, just maybe, my French would have sounded better. I make a mental note to organise rides and vehicle placement close to the stadium for future games. But I go to sleep happy. Winning that match was bloody good and it's great that my coming here has been so warmly received by the public as well as the team.

Tourisme. Sightseeing. I've been looking forward to today — a day trip with the whanau. As we pack up the car and head south to Carcassonne I can't help but feel a little like a schoolboy who's playing truant. It's the rugby season and yet I have a legitimate day off in which to go and do something touristy — and with my family. It's the first time in all my years of rugby this has ever eventuated. I've travelled the world, been to the UK more times than I can quickly count, and yet, despite all there is to see and do in Britain, I've managed to see just three tourist attractions. I toured Edinburgh Castle — twice — and took in a tour of the old Edinburgh city. Third on my list was a visit to Buckingham Palace. That was to meet the Queen. Yeah, I know I'm lucky, it's more than most other people get to do.

But it was all a kind of Clayton's experience — how to tour a foreign country without being a tourist. And it wasn't through a lack of effort on my part; it was due to the lack of free time because of our rugby commitments. When we tour, we are there to play rugby, to do a job, therefore sightseeing isn't part of the agenda. My tourism experiences in Edinburgh took place when I was with the New Zealand Maori squad, tea with the Queen was as an All Black and it was part of a team commitment. Oh, I almost forgot, we did lineouts at the Castle Keep in Cardiff too.

However, that's all in the past and it's exciting to know that although I've spent a considerable amount of time in the northern hemisphere there remains much to see — new countries and regions to explore. Best of all, this time round I'll be enjoying these new experiences with Juanita and the girls.

The trip to Carcassonne doesn't take long and it's impossible not to be impressed as we drive into the car park situated at the foot of this walled Cité. Carcassonne is the only fortified town in Europe that is still inhabited and such is its importance UNESCO declared it a World Heritage site in 1997.

It's amazing to be able to walk through the cobbled streets surrounded by incredibly ancient buildings that are operating as shops, hotels, pubs and housing in the 21st century. We pick our way across the uneven cobbles and traverse the occasional gang-plank, admiring the filled-in moats and old wells and running our hands across the stone walls. We look up at the magnificent Gothic cathedral that dominates the old Cité. It's impossible not to be awestruck by its sheer size, let alone knowing it was built so long ago.

L'histoire. The history. Carcassonne is more than 2000 years old and its history is heavy with long and bloody battles, murders and conquests. Its heyday was at the beginning of the 13th century when it was home to 4000 people, a prosperous place where religious differences were put aside and people were considered to be tolerant of one other. But in 1209 the Crusades began and Carcassonne fell. For a time the county of Carcassonne was under the jurisdiction of Barcelona but when the Viscount of Carcassonne was murdered, to be replaced by one Simon de Montfort, it wasn't long before France laid claim to the city. Under French rule the citadel was strengthened, as were the five fortresses along the Spanish border. These are known today as the 'Five Sons' of Carcassonne.

But the 'Five Sons' could do little to protect the town in 1348 when the Black Plague wiped out almost all the population. There was more bad luck just seven years later when the Lower Town, which is aligned to but situated outside the Cité walls, was completely destroyed by troops of the Black Prince. Taxes and robbers continued to plunder

Le Rugbyman

the region and 100 years later, in 1531, religious differences divided the town, with the Cité remaining Catholic and the rebuilt Lower Town converting to Protestantism. According to the history books, it was an excuse for yet another bloody conflict. But once again the town picked itself up, reinvented its usefulness and became a major player in the textile industry.

Funnily enough, the French Revolution of 1789–99 almost passed Carcassonne by. Maybe they were simply tired of fighting. Or maybe what was happening so far away in Paris was considered of little consequence to the daily lives of Carcassonne's inhabitants.

As it happened, the revolution would impact greatly on the fortunes of Carcassonne because the textile industry faltered in the early 1800s and its eventual but gradual recovery would be too slow and too late for the township. But don't despair. This is a good news story and although the Cité began to fall into disrepair, the French were savvy enough to realise they had a treasure worth saving. In 1849 it was classified as an Historical Monument and restoration work got underway, led by Viollet-le-Duc, a famous French architect. Although the textile industry continued its decline the area got a new lease of life as a wine region. I'll drink to that.

Tourism is also big business. More than three million people visit Carcassonne each year. It's wonderful to be here, to be part of that throng of tourists, just another family enjoying their Sunday outing, seeing the sights and soaking up the medieval atmosphere. It's impossible not to be affected by what we see, especially when you consider the age of this place and its history. It also makes you realise what a young country New Zealand is.

As we wander the streets I am in awe of the manpower that must have gone into building these fortresses, especially when you know it was all done without the aid of modern machinery. The time it must have taken and the generations of families, the tradesmen and labourers who would not have seen the project complete, is hard to fathom.

Eva's level of appreciation is different to Juanita's and mine. As a three year old she thinks the Cité makes an excellent adventure playground, complete with its climbing frame of lots of stairs and pokey holes in the wall in which to play peek-a-boo. Inez, meanwhile, is too young to cultivate an opinion about the sights she sees from the comfort of her parents' arms, or from her pram. I guess for both the girls, given their young years, such trips will be over their heads. But Juanita and I will make great scrapbooks and photo albums for them and through looking at those hopefully our daughters will have a glimpse of their 'first time' experiences, those with a foreign element attached. I hope they come back one day and retrace their preschool and toddler footsteps when they will be able to truly appreciate what they see.

It's been a mind-blowing day. Not only am I surrounded, quite literally, by so much history, I've been a bona fide tourist. It's been a heady experience. We take a different route home, driving through the mountains, which makes the trip longer but it is much more scenic and well worth the effort. We now have more of an idea what is contained within our French backyard. Medieval villages dot the countryside, we spy chateaux perched high up on the edge of cliff faces; farmlets, vineyards, quaint churches and pretty little towns are only a short drive away from Castres. I can't wait until we set off on our next road trip around France. *Je suis content.*

6

Christmas is Coming

La période dês fetes. The festive season. December arrives and I find myself surplus to rugby requirements. The next round of the Heineken Cup is about to get underway and because I joined the Castres' squad part way through the season I am ineligible to play in the competition at this stage. Hopefully the team makes the quarter-finals because I will be able to play from then on. From what I have seen so far, the European Cup provides much stronger competition and at a considerably higher level than what I am experiencing playing in the *Championnat du France*.

But qualifying for the quarters is not something Castres can take for granted because they are in a pool with some formidable opposition — the Neath-Swansea Ospreys from Wales, Harlequins from England and Irish provincial side Munster, who regularly make the semi-finals or finals but have yet to win the tournament. Before

Le Rugbyman

my arrival in France, Castres had a good result at home against the Ospreys, winning 38–17 and then drew 23-all against Harlequins in London. In Round Three we have another home game and it is against the strong Munster unit. To date, they've had two wins for two matches played, beating Harlequins 15–9 at Limerick's Thomond Park (apparently the ground has a reputation similar to Dunedin's House of Pain), and then on the road defeating the Ospreys 20–18.

Because of my ineligibility for European Cup rugby, my family and I take the opportunity to explore the countryside around us a little more. We make the decision to go abroad so to speak, to visit another country. Andorra is only a three-hour drive from Castres. Nestled high in the Pyrénées mountains between France and Spain, this tiny country — land mass 468 square kilometres — reinvented itself after the Second World War through tourism. Over 9,000,000 people visit the country annually, attracted by its duty-free status and its summer and winter resorts. I've done some reading up on the place and found that tourism accounts for 80 per cent of Andorra's gross domestic product. And of the population of just under 70,000, the majority, 43 per cent, is Spanish. Andorrans make up 33 per cent. The country is Catalan-speaking, a language which apparently is more similar to Spanish than French — which means I expect to be able to understand very little! Another thing I find difficult to comprehend, maybe because I come from New Zealand, is that only 2 per cent of land in Andorra is arable. But, there is a plus side — skifields in abundance.

We are planning this trip on a two-pronged basis: a quick overnight stay to suss the place out and then to return the following weekend with Brad Fleming in tow. He's suffered a neck injury that will sideline him for about four weeks.

Thanks to the dream motorway system crisscrossing France, long-distance driving is not a problem and the journey to Andorra is a breeze. Generally, it is safe to travel at speeds of 130 km per hour because the roads are so good. As we reach the mountains of the Pyrénées the route suddenly becomes a little steeper and I have to drop down a gear or two. As I gaze at the towering mountains I am reminded of the drawings I used to do as a child. The mountains resemble a series of triangles, neatly coloured in with different shades of green and all topped off with a cone of white snow. Then, as we wend our way higher into the ranges, it's as if the child artist has run out of enthusiasm, or green pen, and has filled in the triangles with a dull shingle-grey. The mountains are a looming sombre presence and we drive silently onwards, upwards.

I have high hopes that the trip will provide an opportunity to get another stamp in my passport but the border patrols are more than just a little relaxed. By the time I finish wondering what that uniformed bloke is doing standing in the snow and watching cars drive past, I realise I've entered another country. As a border-crossing experience, it's a bit of a let down.

During this brief stopover, however, we see enough to convince us to return the next weekend, and so a week later, and accompanied by Brad, we set off. We are in high spirits, determined to enjoy ourselves. As we climb into the mountains, now following an almost familiar route, the snow on the roadside deepens. We stop for the obligatory stretching of the legs which quickly develops into a snow fight. Unfortunately, in my haste to get into the snow, I forget to don my coat and during the war of snowballs I cop one to the head from Brad. The blow renders me useless as I fall victim to a vicious 'ice-cream' headache and then start shivering violently as the snow slips down my neck. Okay, it might be round one to Brad this time, but he'll keep! The season and the snow are far from finished.

With the sense knocked back into us we continue on our way. The first town we come to is Pas de la Casa. It's a resort-type ski town with, of course, good shopping and we discover that hundreds of people are there before us, taking advantage of the duty free and skiing all in one. Cars line the road as far as we can see and I'm grateful we're carrying on to the main centre, Andorra La Vela.

The main road into the city is also its major shopping street. A few kilometres long, it is jam-packed with people. But we are feeling very relaxed about our visit here. Having done the recce just a week ago we know where we're going, where to eat and specific places to visit. I'm happy we've had the foresight to book accommodation and even happier with the price we end up paying. I've become used to being anonymous, and in fact it makes for quite a nice change after having such a visible visage back in New Zealand. Only recently, Juanita was commenting on how novel it is to be out and about with me and not getting the looks normally reserved for well-known people. Around Castres I have quickly become accepted as one of the locals, more part of the furniture than anyone too special. There's no real fuss made over me when I'm out and about. And here in Andorra, Juanita and I can wander the streets and sit in restaurants and relax over a meal without being stared at. But as we check in to our hotel the bloke at reception asks where we are from.

'New Zealand,' I reply.

He gives me a thoughtful stare. 'You look like *that* rugby player,' he says.

I mumble something like, 'Oh, yeah,' when Juanita pipes up, saying, 'You mean the guy who pokes his tongue out during the haka?'

The guy decides that's exactly who I look like and Juanita happily confirms his suspicions. I refrain from doing the haka but my cheeky grin earns us a huge discount on the price of our room. Anonymity is a good thing, but every now and then being known works in your favour. We enjoy a few quiet drinks at the hotel. And thankfully they are quiet because the next two days are devoted to shopping till we drop. The festive season is definitely upon us.

Faire des courses. Shopping expedition. It's 16 December and a Thursday, my day off. Tomorrow we're moving into our own place and so we decide to take a quick trip to Toulouse and stock up on some household necessities. Although the house we're renting is semi-furnished, and we have a container coming from New Zealand with items that include beds, a sofa and our table and chairs, all our breakables were left behind. It's those things we need to replace and they are top of today's shopping list.

Toulouse is approximately an hour's drive from Castres but it never seems to take that long to get there because the route is so built up — you always seem to be travelling through towns or farmlets. It's one of the major differences between France and New Zealand. Back home, lengthy trips can be made through a countryside that appears to be uninhabited. You can be surrounded by forests, native bush or pastures — vast tracts of land that stretch into the distance, some paddocks dotted with animals, but where humans are hard to find. In France, land is much more intensively farmed. And the French seem to have a national hate of unused space and everywhere you go you see neat rows of crops, often vines, and sometimes planted out on seemingly impossible terrain. The Frenchman may be flamboyant of character but his garden is likely to be an example of military-precision planting:

vegetables and flowers cultivated to within an inch of their lives and all standing to attention — a production line of produce. A garden is about putting food on the table or flowers in a vase, and landscaped gardens full of designer plants would mystify most Frenchmen. What's their point, they would wonder? *Ooh la, la! C'est drôle!*

But back on the road, I'm in confident mood. My previous trips to Toulouse may have been as a passenger but I've received instructions from a team-mate who has ventured into the big smoke many times. It can't be that difficult, can it? However, thanks to my mate's 'excellent' directions we end up circling the city twice before figuring out the route for ourselves. The old saying of 'he who laughs first' bites me in the ass big time. Only yesterday I was taking the mickey out of another team-mate who had spent an hour and a half lost on the roads of Toulouse. Now, here I am with my own snigger lingering in my ears along with the 'flea' my wife's giving me — something along the lines of men, maps and directions!

The problem is that if you are lost in France and speak only pidgin — well, let's be honest here, *no* French — asking for directions at the local gas station is a veritable no-go. Today, I'm frustrated about the hassle with directions and, yeah, my pride is a tad wounded. But, eventually, we are able to get to where we want to go and manage to buy our purchases without any further ado. It's another experience we can mark up: good moments, bad moments. At least we are getting positives as well as negatives.

Safely back in Castres, I receive a phone call from a local reporter wanting to do a story on the Meeuws family's first Christmas in France. He says the paper is putting together a feature on how foreigners in France plan to celebrate *Noël* and wants our perspective on festive celebrations.

Christmas is Coming

On behalf of my family I agree to speak with the journalist. I know I'm taking liberties here because I need Juanita to help me out with interviews. But she doesn't mind acting as interpreter. We work well together as a team.

Le bruit court. Rumour has it. We've never really indulged in the media game so when I drag Juanita in to be a part of the interviewing process it's always with a little trepidation on my part. Early on in our relationship we made the decision not to do the women's magazine thing or to let our lives be splurged across any other forms of media. Our reasoning was simple. We are pretty private people, and in our opinion what goes on in our relationship is between us. The only other people we want to be privy to family matters are — just that — our families and, of course, close friends.

That doesn't mean the press has always respected our decision. In Dunedin we had to endure a couple of occasions when the media decided there were aspects of our lives they were eager to share with the rest of New Zealand. It was either information they'd come across through eavesdropping, chatting to one of my team-mates or trying to state some ridiculous rumour or other as gospel. We managed to diffuse these incidents by choosing to ignore the situation or by saying straight up that that no permission had been granted for anyone to print a two-page spread on us for a feature column in the weekend papers. Thankfully, these times were once-in-a-blue-moon scenarios and there was no need to beef up security! A couple of times we did agree to do a little something for the local paper but those articles were hardly intrusive.

However, once we moved up to Auckland the media business became a whole different ball game. For three years it felt as if I was everywhere. At one stage Juanita said she was sick of seeing me everywhere but at home. I was involved in promos, magazine articles, in newspapers, on billboards, even on the back of a bus, doing TV or radio interviews and taking part in a variety of charity events. Looking back, that publicity circuit contributed to making it a rather crazy three years. Sometimes it felt as if I were a spectator looking in on the life of a rugby player, this bloke who was trying to do no more than lead an ordinary life when he wasn't out training, playing matches or touring with a team. It sure didn't feel like it was my life.

We were fielding phone calls from agents or reporters at all hours of the day and night wanting to photograph, interview or film me with my family. Yes, we were offered money on many occasions but we kept saying no.

One incident nearly caused us to change our minds and made us think seriously about needing to put out in the public domain that I was a family man, happily married and with children. Thanks to the media, and because I was a sportsman, I'd become in the eyes of many, Kees Meeuws, rugby player, an aggressive and hard-ass mongrel.

It is fair comment to say that on the field of play I won't be seen grinning or smiling a lot. It's also true to add that during my career I've been involved in more punch-ups and sendings-off than I care to remember. For people who don't know me, I guess it's reasonable to make the assumption that I'm a tough customer when it comes to my work. But playing rugby is still like any other profession — you have a job to do so you adopt the necessary attitude in order to fulfil your work obligations.

Maybe too, because I'm covered in more moko than the average Joe Blow, images of *Once Were Warriors* were too easy to conjure up for some people. Neighbours and friends were being asked if the police were at my house every other day ending in 'y'! My wife suddenly became this supposed victim because of me. This, plus other tall stories, couldn't have been further from the truth. However, matters came to a head when the police informed me of a crazed fan and it was that which prompted Juanita and me to do something public. The hope was that if I was seen as 'Kees Meeuws — ordinary bloke', it would help quell the stories doing the rounds that I was 'Kees Meeuws — dreadful ogre'.

En réalité. In reality. A production company wanted to film a number of All Blacks doing their thing. A 'Day in the life of Kees Meeuws' was to involve cooking and it was to be done with *Hell's Kitchen* chef Rick Rutledge Manning. Filmed at my home, the programme showed me out hunting, with my family, with friends and there was also a general interview about my life away from the rugby field, the emphasis being on food and health.

After the one-hour programme had gone to air Juanita was happy to note that the media refrained from referring to me as a mongrel. And instead of 'hard man', I became 'rugby hard man Kees Meeuws', or I was said to be someone 'having the mongrel for rugby'.

I was surprised to hear from friends and family — and even my bank manager — that they were asked by many people if the programme portrayed the real Kees Meeuws. It intrigues me that my rugby persona had become so easily attached to the everyday me and I now appreciate how some actors must feel when their fans, or foes, seem unable to separate them from the characters they play.

On reflection, my Otago nickname, Badnewz, may not have helped my cause. But there was nothing sinister about that tag.

Team-mate at the time John Leslie, known as JL, named the front row after characters from the WWF wrestling show. Not because of our off-field antics but because of what we looked like. We were Carl 'Bulldog' Hoeft, Anton 'Hatchet' Oliver and Kees 'Badnewz' Meeuws. That name stuck until I moved to Auckland where the boys gave me a new name, Poppa Bear, something to do with me on a motorbike and the movie *Armageddon*. I like to think Poppa Bear suits me much better than Badnewz.

I became a spokesperson for Women's Refuge and helped to front their 2004 campaign against domestic violence. My father was very strong on the subject of physical abuse: it's a no-no and above all else you don't hit women. Personally, I think men who use their fists against women are committing abuse of the worst kind. In my opinion, guys who resort to such actions are pussies who lack character and self-control.

Another campaign I became involved with was Allergy Awareness. It's something I continue to support because it affects my family and me. It's the one time I've agreed to strip to the waist, and the shot used to promote their 2004 awareness-week campaign shows me holding my infant daughter Inez in my arms. That image appeared on posters and magazine covers throughout New Zealand. Then *What Now* did a Father's Day special and I was invited to appear on the show with my children. Four of my five offspring spent the morning with me doing the show and we had a ball.

I will always be keen to promote the 'be strong, be clean' anti-drug message. I don't believe in the taking of performance-enhancing or illegal drugs and I don't think cheats should prosper.

On a personal level, I've had to face down years of accusations that I was doing drugs. I've been accused of taking stuff because of my size: apparently I was 'always on the 'roids'. It's all rubbish. The rumours started when I was at Kelston Boys when it seemed some people just couldn't accept that my body shape is, well, my body shape! I put my frame down to a combination of two factors — genetics and a lot of hard work in the gym. I was never a small boy so why on earth would anyone imagine I was going to grow up to be a small man?

What's important to me now is that I can use my profile as a rugby player to get the message across to kids that if you do the hard work, the muscles will come. But, if you're prepared to cheat, to take drugs, you run the risk of getting caught out. It would be the ultimate disgrace and there's also the very real possibility that you are harming your body.

I guess my experiences, both good and bad, go to prove that there are times when opening up to the media can be more positive than negative. Allowing the television cameras into my home certainly helped to dispel my mongrel image and through that positive publicity I was invited to support several worthy causes. Courtesy of their powerful messages, I've been able to give something back to the community. It was a two-way street and I am very grateful for the way things turned out.

Nous sommes sur la bonne voie. We are on the right track. It's no secret that Juanita understands a lot more French than I do, and that hers has progressed even more since arriving in France. Her assistance eases the pressure on me during this latest request for a story and it turns out to be a pleasant experience for all involved. It's a nice, easy interview and, as a bonus, it's all about one of my expert subjects — food.

Le Rugbyman

Of course, given the French obsession with food, the reporter wants to know what we will be preparing for Christmas dinner. Wanting to impress, we throw in a few French favourites, starting off with *foie gras*. Literally translated, foie gras means 'fat liver'. The specially bred geese or ducks are force-fed over a four- to five-month period. The fowl are purposely not exercised and, therefore, the combination of over-eating and a sedentary lifestyle results in a huge and fatty liver. Once the bird is killed the liver is soaked overnight in either port, water or milk and then, after further marinating and seasoning, it is baked. Force-feeding of the birds is somewhat controversial these days. But, as the French are ruled by their stomachs, the majority ignore the complaints of the PC brigade and get on with enjoying what is considered a real delicacy. And I have to say that it does taste great — even better if you are prepared to just eat it, not ask what it is, where it's come from and how it was cooked. Sometimes you can get too much information!

Next on our Christmas menu is duck, *le canard*, and after that we'll find it impossible to go past a few treats from the patisserie. The French certainly know how to bake the most amazing tarts and treats. The bonus is that as well as being absolutely delicious they are relatively inexpensive.

A few family snapshots are taken and the reporter goes away happy. What the Meeuwses will be having for Christmas dinner is detailed in the following week's paper.

Le déménagement. Moving house. With one week to go to Christmas, we're finally able to move into our own place, somewhere to call home for the next two to three years. We've been living marae-style on the lounge floor of a team-mate's apartment and then, two nights before the big move, we had to shift once more into another team-mate's place.

We can't get into our own place quickly enough. It's been almost three months since we left our home in Greenhithe and living out of suitcases in a succession of places has taken its toll on all of us in one way or another. Especially the haunted mansion experience. It's all been particularly hard on the girls. They need some sort of permanence and their own space. Talking of space, there's not a lot of it on the street where we live. It's a funny little *rue*, only one car wide at both ends and with a slightly wider area in the middle. It's a dead-end road so good luck to you if you need to turn around. No provision has been made to accomplish that task. I can see my reversing skills getting a lot better between now and the time we move out.

But despite any potential driving hazards, today is a day of great expectations for my family and me. However, rugby still has to take precedence and I have a training session in the morning. With that over I start collecting up our gear which is spread out over three locations. As I make the many trips to collect our belongings, I become increasingly grateful that Castres is a small town — and not just due to moving house. These days it takes me about 10 minutes to travel 10–15 km to trainings and back — and that's in peak traffic. It's a far cry from my days of being cooped up in a car for up to an hour and a half to travel 25–30 km and then still have the return journey to endure. No, I don't miss Auckland traffic!

The move is rushed but goes smoothly. Team-mates are happy to lend a hand. There are our clothes, children's toys and food. Who would have thought such items could be so heavy and that we would have accumulated so much in such a short time? But it feels good to finally be able to put our things away in our own place.

We have a few items we need to purchase. A washing machine is near the top of the list and some kitchen items, but we will tackle those jobs over the next few days. Right now, it's just great to spread out in our home away from home.

Eva thinks so too. We find her in the bathroom having the time of her life. She has discovered the bidet and thinks it is fabulous to have a special toilet where you can do your business and wash your hands all at the same time. The bidet quickly becomes off-limits.

Le match chez nous. A home game. But there is no time to play house. The day after the move I'm back into game mode because we are playing Montpellier. It is a home game and therefore the pressure to win increases. The previous weekend we played away from home, at Pau. To say I was disappointed with our performance is a massive understatement. Okay, it was an away game but Pau was well below us on the championship table. We could have won the match, indeed we should have, but we certainly didn't deserve to — and that's the most annoying aspect of the whole experience. Being French, our guys decided to play down to their expectations. When doing our pre-match drills it was as though everyone was only going through the motions and there was a real lackadaisical attitude to the match. It was if the game had already been played and we were warming down with the result safely in the bag. Unfortunately, it wasn't and we lost 20–29. It's a game that cost us dearly. We slumped three places on the table.

Because we didn't play well I was expecting we'd get a collective rap over the knuckles at our debrief session on the Monday. But it never happened. Instead it was more an attitude of, 'Oh well, yep we lost that one but let's not worry about it'. Sure, everyone was disappointed but they didn't dwell on it; they seemed their same jocular selves and simply set their sights on the next game. The attitude of the French continues to baffle me and it's a far cry from what I'm used to.

But to give them their due, the guys have trained really hard in the lead-up to today's match. Montpellier is also below us on the table, but not so far that we can afford to take them lightly. They are known for their big scrum and much is being made of their Tongan-born, New Zealand-developed loosehead prop, Philemon Toleafoa. He cuts an impressive sight standing 195 cm tall and weighing in at 140 kg. He makes me look small! At 22 years of age he is supposed to be an outstanding rugby prospect and rumours concerning his future abound. According to the local grapevine (later confirmed) he is wanted for France but that he's turned down a contract and instead signed with the NZRU and Waikato. All the talk here is that Graham Henry wants him to return home to play Super 12 so he will become eligible for All Black selection.

The French press have been going overboard about Toleafoa's awesome scrummaging and devastating strength, all the impetus I need to gear myself up for a big game. I'm keen to check him out, to judge for myself whether or not he is a good enough candidate for Super 12 rugby, let alone the All Blacks. And, of course, my pride is at stake here.

As a game, we play 80 pretty uneventful minutes to come away with an 18–10 win. All our points come from the boot of Richard Dourthe and my major frustration is that my team-mates seem quite content to opt for shots at goal rather than trying to score tries. There are the obligatory punch-ups and we win the yellow card count too, in that only one of our players, Romain Froment, gets to spend 10 minutes in the sin bin while Montpellier have two of their players sidelined during the match.

A further plus is that we dominate the much-vaunted Montpellier scrum, and as for testing the young Kiwi fella out . . . well, after the game I wish him luck with his career. I give him some pointers with regard to the Super 12 and what the expectations are within that. I think that if he puts his mind to it he could do well. He's certainly a big boy and he has the potential to be a real asset to New Zealand rugby when he returns home. Unfortunately, we don't get a lot of time to chat. Toleafoa and his team-mates have a six-hour bus ride back to Montpellier. I wonder if they'll be flying to their next away match?

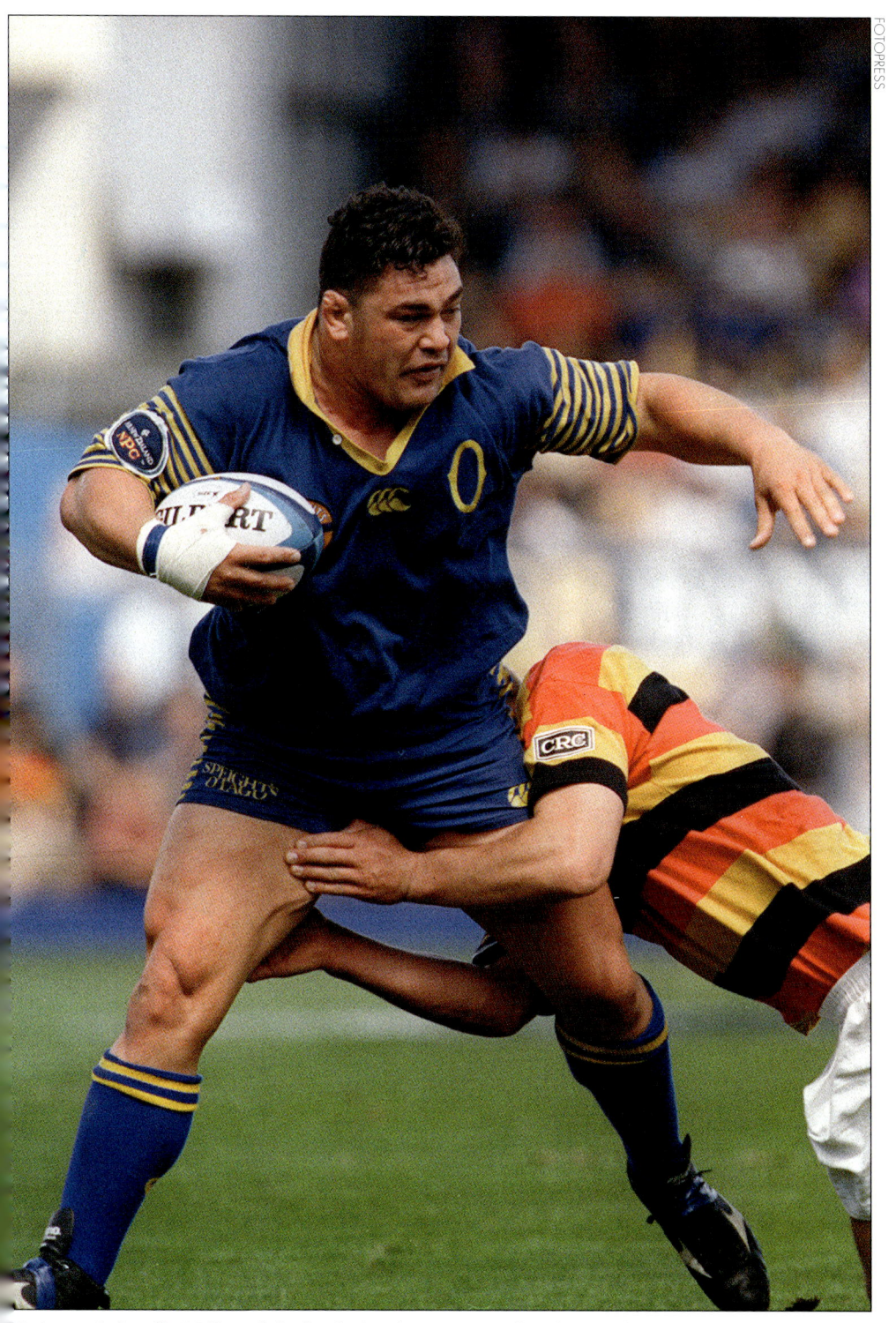

Trying to shake off a Waikato defender during the 1998 NPC first division final at Carisbrook. It was a great game and it capped off a great season. Final score: Otago 49, Waikato 20.

Above: Celebrating with Reuben Parkinson after Otago's victory in the '98 NPC final. Below: How sweet it was . . . with the Otago boys after the win over Waikato at Carisbrook. I'm at the far right of the picture.

Above: Two Queenslanders try to halt my progress during the Highlanders' Super 12 match at Carisbrook in 2000. It was a great start to the season as we smashed the Reds 50–13. Right: Big Bulls prop Jaco Espag tries to hang on as I charge upfield in the 1999 Super 12 match at Invercargill. We won the match 65–23 and went all the way to the final before losing narrowly to the Crusaders.

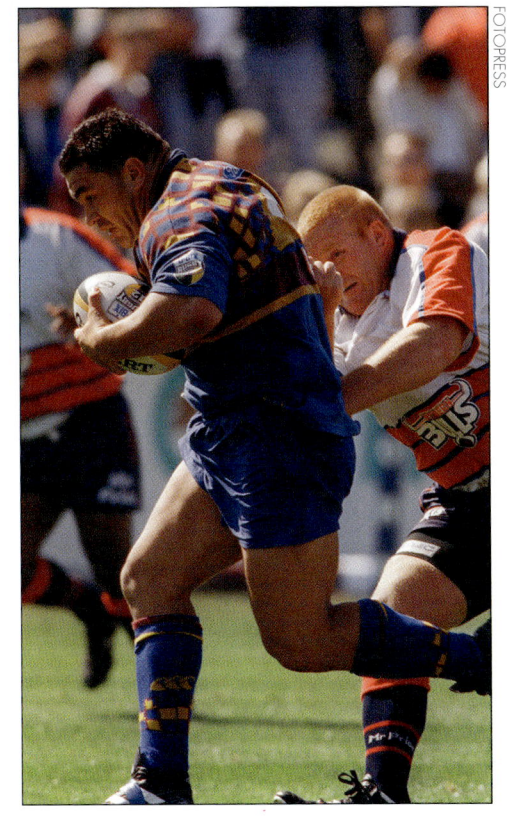

Above: Happy? You bet! This photo was taken moments after the Blues' 21–17 win over the Crusaders in the final of the 2003 Super 12 at Eden Park. Below: Jerry Collins is lining up a big hit on me in action from the Super 12 match between the Blues and the Hurricanes in Wellington in 2004.

Above: A moment to savour. I've just scored for the All Blacks against Canada in a pool match at the 2003 World Cup . . . and I've equalled the world record for the most test tries by a prop. Right: Taking a Welshman for a ride in the All Blacks' 53–37 win over Wales at the 2003 World Cup in Sydney.

The haka has always been special to me. Here the All Blacks challenge the Pacific Islanders prior to the start of the test at Albany in 2004.

FOTOPRESS

I've got England's Joe Worsley in my sights during the All Blacks' 36–12 win over the Poms at Eden Park in the second test of the 2004 series.

The sunnies and the earrings might be fashion accessories, but the tattoos are special, personal expressions of my heritage.

7
Eat, Drink and Be Merry

Je veux en acheter . . . I want to buy some . . . It's five days before Christmas and our home is a flurry of activity. Juanita is busy settling into the house so she sends me on an errand. I have to go into town, to the post office. I am armed with my little French phrase book to help me out and from which I have prepared a sentence to say to the teller at *le bureau de poste*. When I arrive I trot out my phrase: '*Je voudrais quatre timbres pour Nouvelle Zélande s'il vous plaît,*' which translates as 'I would like four stamps for New Zealand please'. Holy hell, she understands me!

Errand complete and flushed with success, not to mention a sudden burst of confidence, I make rapid plans. Now that I can speak French, I'll move on and get some other chores done. First stop is the TV shop where I want to purchase a television set and organise cable television. No problems there, and my mission is successfully completed. Feeling invincible, I set off for France Telecom to organise the phone and internet connection. The guy in the shop speaks and understands some English so it seems to be a walk in the park. In fact, I'm beginning to feel like a local.

Completing the post office errand and managing to get other tasks done makes my day. I also earn a good number of brownie points when I return home and relate my accomplishments to Juanita. It's a nice feeling to bask in the glory of a successful day and I'm confident everything will be connected and up and running over the next couple of days.

Two days later I come back to earth with a massive bump. Juanita spends the entire day sorting out French Telecom and cable TV. It seems as though my French wasn't as flash as I'd thought. Bugger. But I did buy those stamps! Small steps . . . small steps.

Un bon cadeau. A good gift. Christmas is almost here but I still have a job to do before I can immerse myself in festive celebrations. It is the 23rd and we have a home game against Agen. I am looking forward to the match for a couple of reasons. Several of the opposition team are well-known to me; in fact they are my former Blues team-mates Rupene Caucaunibuca, Vula Maimuri and Christian Califano. It will be one thing to catch up with them during the game but hopefully we can indulge in a little Christmas cheer afterwards because when the referee blows the whistle to signal fulltime we begin a 10-day break from rugby.

I am expecting a tough encounter. Agen need a win. They lie in eighth place to our fourth but they have a strong side and apparently rate their chances of snatching a victory, despite the fact they have to do it on the battleground of Castres' Stade Pierre Antoine. Agen are strong up front and have an electric backline thanks to players of the calibre of Rupene and a few others with lots of gas in their tanks. However, our motivation is strong. We want to cement our place in the championship's top four. It promises to be a tough match for both teams.

As I expect, the Agen scrum is very good. Christian is a real rugby warrior and plays exactly as you'd expect the most-capped test prop in France to perform. He may have retired from the international scene but he is still a formidable unit. His front row propping partner is a certain Jean-Jacques Crenca, another tough customer. Jean-Jacques and I have locked horns before. He helped earn me a yellow card in the 2002 All Blacks versus France match. Played at Stade de France, the honours were shared that November day — 10-all at halftime and finishing up 20–20.

My yellow card was the first of three dished out to the All Blacks during the course of the match. I was sent to the sinbin in the 10th minute for what one report said was 'a backslap to the opposition prop (Crenca) out of the scrum breakdown'. The inference from the article was that Australian referee Scott Young was a little overzealous with that ruling but it was a tactic the ref continued to employ enthusiastically throughout the match. Christian Califano was sinbinned in the 30th minute for a professional foul and Mark Robinson found himself cooling his heels on the sideline 10 minutes later after being charged with retaliation. It seemed like it was revolving doors out there.

Fortunately, with Castres, we hold things together well. Prior to the match our coaches had expressed concern that we may have already gone on holiday — mentally. But the boys front up and I rate our performance as one of the best since I've been here.

Okay, we still don't score any tries but we win quite comfortably, 18–6. Richard Dourthe kicks three penalties and our first-five, *notre demi d'ouverture,* Yann Delaigue, is on target with three dropped goals. Yann, 32, is in his first season with Castres and he came to us from arch-rivals Stade Toulouse. His experience certainly helps guide us to victory today.

I'm especially pleased with my own form, no doubt spurred on by opposing Christian in the first half, and when he moves to tighthead in the second spell I am propping against Jean-Jacques. My work rate is huge and during the match I touch the ball 18 times. For a front-row forward to be so involved in the game is almost unheard of in France. I also put in some really big tackles.

The result and the way I play are a huge relief. I finally feel as though I understand how the French play this game. More importantly, I dominate my position. While trying to find my rugby feet over here it's been the one aspect of my game I worried I'd lost some control over. It's nice to get it back. After the game it's obvious my coach is pleased too. It has been, as they say, a good day at the office.

Later on I manage to catch up with my mates from Agen. It's bloody good to see them and to share our experiences of French rugby. They confirm my feelings to date and tell me that the second season is a lot easier than the first. It's reassuring news.

Christian is in good form and it's great seeing him in his own environment. He tells me to give him a call and says he will invite us to dinner sometime soon.

Eventually we make our way to *La Grillade* where once again Jacques impresses me with his excellent food and wine. It turns into a big night — just one of many we anticipate enjoying during this festive period.

Eat, Drink and Be Merry

La vielle de Noël. Christmas Eve. We have a dinner engagement. Our hosts are our real estate agent and her husband, Laurence and Bruno Delpino. Laurence has been a gem, not only for me but for several of my team-mates as well, an absolute saving grace on many occasions. She seems only too happy to go into bat for us when needed.

Apart from helping us to find a house, Laurence came to my rescue soon after I arrived in France when things I'd expected to be already organised had been left for me to sort out. Now I know that I'm a big boy and I don't expect to be spoon-fed, but there is a level of assistance required when you are new to a country, let alone a foreign-speaking one. The club manager might have been happy to let me organise the opening of bank accounts, my vehicle and accommodation, but quite frankly those tasks were well beyond my capabilities. And then when it came to renting a property! Once again we were left on our own to cope with the organising of a telephone connection, electricity, gas — in fact pretty much everything you associate with moving into a new house.

It's been quite a learning curve. But I know now that I have to spell out *exactly* what I need help with or organised when I'm dealing with the club manager. It's not that the French are trying to make things awkward deliberately; instead it is about the attitude of this particular fella, which is frustratingly *laissez-faire*.

Fortunately, Laurence has been there to help smooth the sometimes rather choppy waters of foreign culture, and over the months we've got to enjoy her and her husband's company. Bruno is a top bloke. Of Spanish descent, he speaks French, Spanish and English. That's impressive in anyone's language. Over the last couple of months he and I have become regular features at the local bar and I get the impression our social paths will continue to cross on a frequent basis.

Juanita and I are looking forward to this evening out. Our instructions are to arrive at 9.30 pm because we won't be eating until after 10 pm and we have been told to expect a traditional French dinner. As to the protocol of accepting a dinner invitation, we aren't too sure about French customs and what we should take along. After some discussion, Juanita and I decide to do the traditional Kiwi thing and so we buy presents for the children, Luca, 11, and nine-year-old Elia, and select a bottle of bubbles and some fine chocolates for their parents. It turns out that our choices are right on the button. They are all thrilled and as a bonus I now have two new young fans of rugby thanks to the Playstation games we took as *les cadeaux*.

The French way of dining is very different to what we are used to in New Zealand. They go in for a lot more courses than we would have back home. The norm here is three, but depending on the occasion, four, five or six-course meals are not uncommon.

Tonight we begin with champagne, which is often served as an *apéritif* in its own right prior to a meal. Then we move on to the *hors-d'oeuvres* which consist of savoury-type cakes, salted *canard* skin and dehydrated nuts, and fish cakes, salmon and caviar served on slices of bread and a spicy snack mix.

Good food is a great relaxer and as we eat our way through this first course we find that the conversation flows easily and it is punctuated by lots of laughter. When we get stuck for words there is no embarrassment. We simply consult a handily placed dictionary, and of course we have Bruno and Juanita helping out with translations.

Next up are fresh oysters, prawns and bread. Being a fella who enjoys my kaimoana I was more than happy to tuck into this course and to quaff down the white wine on offer. Drinking wine here is proving to be something of a learning experience. Back home I would buy wine depending on my or our guests' preference, be it a chardonnay or a sauvignon blanc, a merlot or a pinot. But in France the choosing of a wine is a more complex procedure. For example, the Midi-Pyrénées is a geographical region that produces a variety of wines — whites, *les blancs*, reds or *rouges* and the rose, *rosé*. The labels on the bottles from the region will not necessarily inform you of the grape used and therefore sampling is the only way to work out whether or not it is to your liking. Does it resemble the full-bodied *Bordeaux* or is it more like a *Côte du Rhône*, still a red but much lighter to the palate? I'm well aware that I'm still some way from being a true connoisseur of wine but from my limited experience I know something — they're all bloody good!

But back to the banquet. Post-seafood comes *le foie gras*, which is served on a bed of salad and eaten with bread, *le pain*, in this region pronounced 'parn'. After the goose liver, which has been, of course, accompanied by wine, we move on to a dish of stuffed *capon*. Apparently it's a rooster that's been castrated (ouch) and then fattened. In taste it is similar to a roast chicken — but it's much bigger. This course is washed down with more wine.

Just as I'm beginning to struggle with the amount of food and wine consumed our hosts inform us that we still have dessert, dried fruit and *le café* to go. Groaning inwardly, I make a vow to pace myself better in future. Dining out in France can be an experience of marathon proportions. Did I say that? I'm not so sure that anything physical, especially running, is a good meal-time analogy. Neither am I confident I'll be able to move after this one is over!

Le Rugbyman

Fortunately, we get to sit and chat for a while, letting our stomachs settle before embarking on dessert. It looks spectacular — a chocolate ice-cream log with a honey caramel centre and topped with pretty present decorations. It's a traditional French Christmas dessert, a *bûche de Noël*, a yule log. Of course, I have to sample some and it is delicious. Eventually we have coffee, along with the dried fruit. Apparently it acts as a digestive. It is now two in the morning and both our baby girls are crashed out in our hosts' bed. I feel like joining them.

Eating late is common in France but it sure takes some getting used to. As Kiwis, we are used to a dinnertime ranging between 5 pm and 8 pm (and 8 pm is considered late in our household). But over here the days are structured differently. People often start work between 9.30 and 10 am and then stop for two to two and a half hours during the middle of the day for their siesta. That's also when they have their main meal of the day. And after eating well they have time to take a nap. Work resumes about 3 pm and they don't finish up until 6–7 pm, when they go home and eat again. But this time only lightly. They must be doing it right because I haven't seen many obese French people. There must be something in their carbs-protein loading early in the day — and in the wine. Without making any effort, I've lost five kilos since my arrival here.

Or maybe I've put it all back on thanks to mine hosts! At about 2.30 am we call it a night. Or should that be day? It's Christmas Day and we've got a big lunch to prepare for in a few hours time. Not that food is sounding all that tempting right now!

But we go home happy. We've enjoyed an excellent night out, one we will never forget. Our first Christmas in France without our families doesn't seem quite as lonely as we'd anticipated thanks to the

Eat, Drink and Be Merry

generous hospitality of our hosts, not to mention the vast quantities of food and wine. Yes, we're having a very merry Christmas.

Joyeux Noël. Happy Christmas. Well . . . maybe. We get up late and two of the Meeuws' household are feeling rather seedy. We're all exhausted. The girls had a broken sleep and I feel as though I've hardly had any. But we make an effort to enter into the spirit of Christmas. Eva is aware that Santa, or *Père Noël* as he's known over here, stopped by last night and she is keen to see if there are any treats under the tree with her name on them. It's my baby Inez's first Christmas and she gets quite excited about the brightly coloured wrapping paper and the noise it makes. We take lots of photos and make a video we can send to family back home.

A good present for our families is a Sky TV programme that's shown in New Zealand on Christmas Day. Earlier this month I arrived at training to be told by the coach that a television crew would be filming me and then following me around Castres capturing a day in the life of Kees Meeuws. It's to be televised worldwide.

I was introduced to a sports journalist from Toulouse. No doubt he got the assignment due to the fact he is a fluent English speaker. Filming began immediately and it was pretty weird due to the fact they just followed me around with a camera, not asking or saying anything.

When training was over they accompanied me to lunch. A few of the team agreed to come with me and I phoned Juanita and asked her to come along and to bring the girls. We were all filmed eating and chatting and after the meal we went to Jacques Deen's apartment where Jacques, Brad Fleming and I were interviewed. And that was that.

Although we'd had no opportunity to prepare for the cameras, the programme is well received. Our families view it as they eat their Christmas dinner, crying and laughing as they watch the four of us, happy and grateful to be able to see us settling into our new life in France.

We've invited several team-mates for Christmas lunch plus some of their family members, and a few other team-mates have promised to drop by later on. We stick to our planned menu although we borrow a few ideas from last night's dinner with our new friends, such as how to serve the *foie gras* and how to present certain dishes. We also feel more confident about what wines to serve with which foods.

Our meal is a great success, a good mix of New Zealand and French dining. We don't stagger the courses like the French do and instead place it all on the table Kiwi style and let our guests help themselves to whatever they like and in whatever order they choose. As usual, we have far too much kai.

It's a late night that just keeps getting later. People turn up at all hours to help us celebrate the day. It's great. We haven't had time to get morose and spending our first Christmas so far away from home has turned out to be an enjoyable experience that far exceeds our expectations. That the temperature is around −1°C helps add to the novelty factor. Maybe we'll see snow before the year is out.

Juanita est malade. Juanita is sick. It's Boxing Day and we start sorting out the furniture that came with the house because our own container-load of household effects is due to arrive in five days' time. But I am worried about Juanita. She has a fever and I don't think she is very well. We spend the day quietly, all of us catching up on some much-needed sleep.

But the rest doesn't help Juanita and the next day she is really ill. I must get her to a hospital. Friends rally around and take care of the girls for us. We don't have a family doctor and unfortunately the team doctor is away on holiday. Although Juanita can normally communicate reasonably well, right now she can scarcely breathe. What is going to happen at the hospital when I try to speak French? It all adds to the stress.

But our worries are eased almost as soon as we arrive at the hospital. Juanita manages to puff out a few phrases as to how she is feeling and the hospital staff, cottoning on to the limitations of our French language skills, take up the conversation in pidgin English.

I would like to add here, briefly, that we are often asked if we are *Anglais*, English. I have learned to respond immediately with, '*Non, Nouvelle-Zélande*' or '*Néo-Zélandais, et je parle anglais*'. People warm to you as soon as you mention New Zealand. The French have a soft spot for us Kiwis whereas they can be quite hostile if they think you are English. Being a rugby player helps out too. But I digress . . .

Juanita is a chronic asthmatic and I think the succession of winters has taken a toll on her physically. She has made the diagnosis that she is suffering from a preliminary chest infection and she promptly informs the physician at the hospital of her condition, what she has been taking medicine-wise and then adds that she is a nurse by profession. This final piece of information seems to add the necessary authority to her words and she is quickly hooked up to some breathing apparatus, given a dose of steroids, an x-ray and a hefty prescription to go home with.

Meanwhile, I help out by posing for photographs and signing autographs with everyone, or so it seems, who walks through the hospital doors. I am thankful Juanita's condition isn't too serious otherwise my posing for photos with the local population could be construed as quite macabre. Or maybe it's just the French way and they don't get too fazed by illness. *C'est la vie* and all that. Nothing surprises me with the French.

But there are positives to be taken from what has been a worrying time. The French hospital staff are attentive and helpful and my fear of not being able to communicate in a crisis situation has eased somewhat. It helps to normalise life in France to some degree. But, best of all, Juanita is going to be fine.

Bonne année. Happy New Year. We have a party planned for New Year's Eve. I was worried we may have had to cancel because of Juanita being sick but she is recovering well and we decide to go ahead with it, despite the fact that our furniture from New Zealand has still not arrived. We have a dock strike in Marseilles to thank for this apparently. So, it may be cold, freezing in fact, and our house all but devoid of furniture, but we are determined that tonight's party will be a raging success.

We've chosen a theme, 'Return to the 80s' — our inspiration being the rather garish 1980s decor that pervades our house (and yes, we plan to bring it into the 21st century sometime soon). Our guests, a group of mainly expat English-speakers and their kids, are enthusiastic about the idea of a themed party, which of course puts a bit of pressure on the Meeuwses as hosts. It means we have to organise costumes as well as all the food and drink.

It's not every day I find myself hunting through the women's clothing section of the supermarket but Juanita and I have decided to dress up as a Richard Simmons ensemble. Do you remember the guy? He was the fuzzy-haired weight loss and fitness guru from the

Eat, Drink and Be Merry

United States. He attracted a massive television audience and put out videos in the mid-80s under such riveting titles as *Platinum Sweat*, *Blast off the Pounds* and *Dance your Pants off*.

So why are we in the supermarket? Because — and the reason is unknown given that France is supposedly a world leader when it comes to fashion — in this country they still make clothes that are pure 1980s. Today, leg warmers are top of our shopping list and we know we'll be able to find them here. Unfortunately, though, they only make them in women's sizes. Is that going to present me with a problem? I'll have to rely on Juanita to be my stylist.

Eventually we stagger home with the fruits of our shopping expedition: bad wigs, sweatbands, the ubiquitous leg warmers and bike pants plus kai for the evening meal. Eva and Inez are delighted with the streamers and balloons we hang around the house. Goodness knows what they will make of our costume efforts!

Ce que c'est amusant! What fun! Our first guests to arrive are Paul Volley and his family, including his brother and sister-in-law who are over from England. They come dressed as the Village People and enter the house to the beat of 'Macho Man'. Next is Glen Metcalfe and his wife. They've gone for the big hair look and strut in wearing rolled-up jeans and satin numbers. South African Jacques Deen and his partner come as Sex Pistols' lead singer Sid Vicious and Madonna (an unusual combination) and Brad Fleming is, I think but don't actually ask, the dark-haired guy from Wham! and his wife Adele, Molly Ringwald. Needless to say, we have a great time. There is a lot of food and alcohol consumed. And that's before some of our French guests turn up.

Now the French don't do drunk. In fact, generally speaking they are extremely restrained when it comes to their consumption of alcohol. Therefore you can imagine the looks on their faces when they are confronted by a house-load of Antipodeans and various other native English-speakers who are neither dressed in what could even be remotely considered chic attire nor particularly coherent due to the large amounts of booze taken on board.

There is a momentary lull in proceedings as polite introductions are made and our four French friends hand over their gifts of expensive chocolates and a *mathusalem* of champagne. They take in our regalia and comment that we are nicely, if oddly, dressed, rather 1980s in fact. *Qui l'aurait dit? Who would have thought it!*

They agree that, yes indeed, the 1980s sense of style remains strong with a certain section of the French population. We find their comments amusing and they regard us as hilarious which means, fortunately, that a potential cultural faux pas is avoided. It's party time and everyone can't help but have fun. We sing 'Auld Lang Syne' and all loop arms and sway to the music, exchanging 'Happy New Years' and '*Bonne années*'.

Then we play some Kiwi music and Poi-E gives the sound system a good workout. Everyone piles into the lounge to bust a move. And bust a move I sure do. During the breakdance sequence of the song I decide to do the 'robot' and finish with a backspin. Now remember, copious amounts of liquor have been enjoyed by this stage but, I hasten to stress, I did warm up with some stretches! However, on my way down to the backspin, I pull my hamstring! I'm suffering equal doses of pain and horror, but as I struggle up, moaning, I find myself laughing at the antics of Brad, especially when he tweaks his injured neck attempting to imitate my backspin. Crocked, the two of us end up sitting the rest of the song out and watch as everyone else successfully manages to perform a backspin.

Eat, Drink and Be Merry

In typical tradition we do the haka to welcome in the New Year. It never ceases to amaze me how much the haka intrigues other cultures and how they love to see it performed.

It is a big night all right. As I eventually make my way to bed I see bodies strewn about in the spare rooms. It is six o'clock on New Year's Day and I've just finished making a few phone calls home. France Telecom will be pleased — in profit already and the New Year only a few hours old. *Bonne fête* and *bon soir*.

New Year's Day I come down to earth with a bump. *J'ai mal de tête*! My head is hurting and so is my hamstring!

8
A New Year

L'hiver. Winter. Despite everything dressed in shades of grey, Castres is a beautiful place and its charm is evident despite the leaden skies and bare-limbed trees that symbolise winter. Our new home town is reminiscent of all things French as described in either books or in movies and photographs. We wander down cobblestone streets and gaze at the ancient buildings. Some are adorned with intricate wrought-iron window boxes that will no doubt have brilliantly coloured geraniums spilling from them in a few months' time. Most of the buildings have shutters on their windows and doors, making it impossible to peer inside, which is frustrating from our point of view because the imposing size and elaborate decorations of some doors hint at grand houses or rooms hidden within.

As with all French towns there are wide and attractive boulevards, but on occasion we find ourselves driving carefully along narrow alleys to find that the road virtually disappears. It is then that a three-point turn is required in order to make it round the next corner. Patience and a degree of skill are required.

The car never gets out of second or third gear as we travel around the *centre ville*. And as a city centre goes it's quite pretty and contains all the things you would expect to find — an ancient and Gothic-looking church, museums and a town hall. Then there is a collection of rather grand-looking buildings that have stood the test of time and many changes of ownership over the years. Former bath-houses are now hotels, old hotels have become museums and the police station was apparently an art gallery in a previous era. The shopping is good and it requires a strong will to pass by some of the pretty peek-a-boo boutiques with their very French wares.

Beautiful but tiny gardens are dotted around the city, adding a welcome splash of colour and a perfect foil to the omnipresent grey-walled buildings. The majority of the buildings are three or four storeys high and butted up tightly against one another, joined at much more than just the hip. The lack of advertising hoardings is in sharp contrast to New Zealand. There is no maiming of shop corners, exterior walls or the countryside by garish billboards and posters.

The river Agout runs through Castres, bisecting the city from north to south. Houses line the river, their upper storeys often hanging out over the water. These same houses have cellars that open out onto the river where, I suppose, boats or ferries moored during the period when Castres was a thriving merchant town. Like much of France, Castres has a long and complicated history, religion, peace and war affecting the town's fortunes — ebbing and flowing — like the river running through it. According to my reading, Castres, once a Roman

A New Year

encampment, was pretty much founded around a Benedictine abbey during the seventh century. It became a centre of some importance, especially around the 12th and 13th centuries when it was renowned for its textile industry. These days, although textiles remain the key to the city's commercial success, it is also known for its manufacturing, pharmaceutical, furniture and machine tool industries.

Sport, education and the arts also flourish here. And that the townspeople revere their sport has been acknowledged at the highest level. In the mid-1990s Castres was named the 'most sporting town in France' due to it having 130-something clubs. I have no idea just what sports are listed on what is an obviously long inventory but locals are justifiably proud of their city's achievement. The claim is that 26 per cent of the resident population is involved in some form of sport, and rugby is one of its best performers. It is a real positive to be living and playing in a city that has such a strong sporting ethos.

Être dans le mouvement. To be in the swim. Huge parks are situated at the northern and southern ends of Castres. We spend a lot of time here because they contain many playgrounds that our girls adore. In summer these parks will pulse with aquatic activity — sailing, kayaking, swimming and fishing. There's a huge swimming complex that the locals of this inland region refer to as their beach; and this is where I discover yet another quaint French custom — that speedos are the regulation *vêtements* for blokes.

Heaven help you if you don't abide by this rule. The French seem to have a curious, and may I venture odd, suspicion of anything that looks like surf shorts. Maybe it's another case of 1980s fashion rearing its ugly head! And as if speedos aren't enough to cope with, there is also that other peculiarly French convention to overcome: their complete lack of modesty. The changing rooms at the swimming pool are mixed. Picture this scene if you will, me trying to squeeze myself into a rather small cubicle so that I can then squeeze myself into my speedos while also trying to change Inez and barking orders at Eva *not* to run away!

Au bord de la mer. At the seaside. We decide to take a trip to the real sea and head for Beziers, a drive of one and a half hours from Castres. Juanita and I are keen to dip our toes into the Mediterranean and that it happens to be the middle of winter cannot dampen our enthusiasm for a day out.

We enjoy a drive that can only be described as stunning. France is such a spectacularly beautiful country no matter what the season. The villages and towns we pass through are superb and if our alcohol-laden New Year celebrations weren't still fresh in my mind, stopping off at one or several vineyards along the route would be high on my to-do list.

Beziers is lovely. Apparently it started off as a coastal town but over the centuries a build-up of sediment meant it had to be moved 13 km inland. From the town we head to the coast. One of the major surprises is the balmy 17°C conditions — a far cry from the −3°C temperatures we are experiencing in Castres.

This is the first trip to a beach for Inez. Aged almost one, her main interest is eating everything she sees in front of her and this includes sampling French sand and shells. The beach obviously reminds Eva of home and she chats about New Zealand as she builds sandcastles.

It's a relaxing time for us all. We cast off our socks and shoes and I roll up my trousers and enjoy the warmth of the sun on my bare skin. But our attempt at sunbathing earns us some strange looks from any locals who walk by, all in their thick winter garb. No doubt they hear us talking in English and are happy to dismiss us as *les étrangers fous*, crazy foreigners.

Jardin d'enfants. Kindergarten. It is a big day in our household. The third of January and Eva is about to start school. It is an emotional day for Juanita and me as we accompany our elder daughter to the place where from now on she will spend four days a week — Mondays, Tuesdays, Thursdays and Fridays. Wednesdays here are always an official day off and although there are classes on Saturdays we think Eva is too young to cope with a full five-day school week.

Her school day starts bright and early at 8.30 am and she will be there until half-past four. The students have a siesta for two hours during the middle of the day. After much discussion we've decided not to bring Eva home for lunch each day. We think it will disrupt her day too much and we aren't completely confident we will always be able to persuade her to return to school for the afternoon session!

It's a tiny private school, apparently up and running for the last 400 years, and it caters for children aged from two and a half up to 13 years. It's also rather forbidding. High walls enclose the complex and the only way in is through either a huge gate that has attic offices above it (many years ago they must have served as gatekeepers' quarters but they now house the principal's office and administration area) or there is a newer side door. Again, like so much of our current environment, everything is grey — such a stark contrast to the schools we know in New Zealand with their lush green playing fields and murals brightening up the outsides of the classroom blocks.

Le Rugbyman

But it's not all bad. Eva's actual classroom has a lot of colour in it and that makes me feel much more comfortable about sending my baby here each day. I've read that the French aren't particularly taken with the idea of children just playing and that they prefer to cram little heads with facts from as young an age as possible. This concept makes more sense when I look around the school. Where are the rugby fields, the soccer pitches and the netball courts? What about just plain grass?

Kindergarten French style, with its structured classes, is going to be a huge leap into the unknown for our daughter. After all, Eva is just a typical three year old. Three! It's hard to fathom that she is about to start school. Despite the fact that Eva is excited, I'm a little nervous on her behalf because not only is she starting her education in a rather formal environment, she will also have to cope with being immersed in the French language and culture. As we walk her to school on that first day, my feelings are similar to the ones I experience when I throw Eva into the deep end of the swimming pool. I am keeping my fingers crossed in the hope that she will swim rather than sink.

And Eva starting school is not the only momentous event of the day. Our furniture from New Zealand is due to arrive after its rather protracted journey around the world. It seems that our goods have stopped off at every imaginable port between New Zealand and France. What a pity we weren't able to accompany them on their global tour. Unfortunately, I have to run. A training session beckons. As I head out the door, Juanita, knee-deep in boxes and bubble-wrap, makes a comment about some things never changing and how she has to do the unpacking every time we shift. Ah, the benefits of rugby, I sigh as I escape to the car. Sorry hon.

A New Year

Incapable d'expliquer. At a loss to explain. I have an enforced two-week break from rugby after Christmas because of the Heineken Cup competition. Castres has a home game against NEC Harlequins early January, and the match is something of a revelation. It's a beautiful winter's day, cool but clear, and our guys respond to the conditions by playing out of their skins to crush Harlequins 58–13. The team puts together some great scoring moves that are rather reminiscent of Super 12 rugby, and the continuity of the game is the best I've witnessed since being in France. I feel very encouraged by what I see.

But a week later everything changes when the boys let themselves down big time. Castres travel to Wales to play the Neath-Swansea Ospreys, a team they beat 38–17 at home in October, just over a month before I arrived in France. There is a lot riding on this second meeting between the sides. Castres are lying second in Pool Four behind Munster and to advance to the quarter-finals, at which stage I can become a participant rather than just a spectator, we need a good win, one that includes getting a bonus point.

As it turns out, the game — the result and the way we play — is a bitter disappointment. It is wet, cold and miserable at The Gnoll and our guys play rugby to mirror the conditions. We are never in the hunt for that vital bonus point either and can manage only one try, from prop Alessio Galasso. Our hopes of European glory are dashed for another season. I am bitterly disappointed. My English-speaking team-mates sum up the performance by saying, 'No one turned up to play rugby.'

I can't work out why the French go dog when the sun isn't shining. It's almost as though they sulk when conditions are less than perfect and they seem to lose their heart to play. It's the same when they travel away to games — they're already convinced the team is going to lose. Add to that mix the mindset adopted when we are playing against teams placed well below ours on the table. Apparently, we only have to turn up to win those games! I wish it were that easy.

I have discovered one thing, though, that is the same the world over. When there is a problem in a team people tend to look outside for excuses rather than looking inwards at themselves. It's an attitude that never ceases to amaze me.

I'm not exactly sure what went wrong in Wales, or what's going down at the club. Whether it's because some of the players and the coaching staff are coming off contract and can't think of anything else . . . I just don't know. The only thing I am sure about is that because I can't speak or understand French all that well I'm only getting half the story. But it's obvious that something is going on.

Être d'accord. To be in agreement. Since my arrival at Castres, it's been organised so that I meet with our forwards coach Christophe Urios every four to six weeks. It's a somewhat comical affair because he doesn't speak any English and my French is limited to say the least. To get our points across we both engage in that typical French habit, much gesticulating, and armed with a whiteboard marker we take turns to frantically draw the points we are trying to make to one another. Thankfully, when written or drawn, rugby is a universal language and we are able to make some headway.

Christophe is a huge fan of the All Blacks' style of play. He appreciates my input and is always receptive to any suggestions I make. Of course, anything I have to say carries more weight thanks to the thumping the All Blacks gave France last November. It's fair to say the French were in awe of the All Blacks after that performance.

A New Year

My Castres team-mates thought they were incredible and the week following the test Christophe kept going on and on about how brilliant the All Blacks were. I saw my chance and didn't waste the opportunity to share some tips, views and info regarding our first team's lineouts and structure at ruck and maul time. Fortunately, Christophe was more than willing to listen and he implemented my suggestions into our trainings and game plan.

In my opinion, our lineout was too simple. We had three jumpers and they all just jumped straight up. Opposing teams knew this and would steal our ball. The end result was that we were losing about 50 per cent of our own ball — far too much.

The changes I suggested gave each jumper three or four jump options. It was therefore up to the individual to calculate what jumping tactic would best beat the opposition, thus taking the stress off the hooker and placing it back on the jumper. Thankfully, this change of tactic has worked. We've made huge improvements and have been winning all our own ball.

It feels good to know I've been able to suggest changes to the way we play that have had an immediate and positive effect on our game. It makes me wonder, though, that if the result in Paris had been different, if France had beaten the All Blacks or even got close to them on the scoreboard, whether or not my input would have been so well received.

As an example of how things might have been, one of the guys in our team had spent the last two years trying to change the way we execute a drive from lineouts, what we call a shifter drive as opposed to a normal drive. Bear with me while I explain the difference.

A normal drive is when, after securing the ball, the lineout jumper comes down and a player goes straight on to him, takes the ball off him and everyone gets in behind and drives on the ball carrier and the blocks (the lifters) all the while moving forward. A shifter drive is the same, except that when the lineout jumper comes down he passes the ball two places behind him and a player goes straight onto the ball in the new position, hence changing the starting point of the drive. It makes it difficult for the opposition to anticipate the start of the drive and for them to disrupt it before it has begun.

Anyway, normal or shifter drive, my team-mate's suggestions had fallen on deaf ears. Then I come along, offer up exactly the same info and *voilà*, at the next training we are learning the new move.

I like to think that these meetings are productive for both coach and player. Christophe is a good man and a good coach and I like the way he is open to new ideas or suggestions.

Perdu dans la traduction. Lost in translation. I knew the language and the rugby here were going to provide me with challenges, but my inability to communicate well is one of my major frustrations. That, coupled with the team's bewildering habit of switching off at trainings, is really getting to me.

I try to get the message across and my spiel goes something like this: 'Hey! You've gotta f**** concentrate at trainings and not throw 50/50 passes!' This is all delivered in a loud and deliberately aggro voice, you know, the 'don't mess with me' tone. Then, in more measured tones, I ask our captain Mario to translate for me. But, despite my efforts, I don't think the message is getting through.

In most ways the French style of rugby is what I expected it to be, all about their passion and flair. But I am baffled by their unwillingness to do the groundwork necessary to achieve the type of game they want to play. This attitude is borne out on the field of

A New Year

play where they can be unbelievably schizophrenic, world-beaters one day and woeful the next.

Throughout my career I've heard much about not being able to predict the French in regard to their game plan or how they will perform. Always play your best game against the French because you can never be certain when they are going to turn up and really play: that's the advice coaches have always handed down. And, believe me, I know what they are talking about, having been on the receiving end of that 43–31 infamous 1999 World Cup semi-final defeat. Yeah, let's *not* go there!

I was a little frustrated at not being able to go up to Paris to watch the All Blacks last November, but I had a club match to play. My own experience that day couldn't have been more different from the buzz the boys in black must have got from their performance.

Our match at Pau and losing 20–29 marked my first real lesson in French attitude towards playing away from home and towards a team that they should dominate. I figure I have many lessons to learn and events to analyse. At times my new life seems bewildering.

I am happy for the All Blacks that they ended their 2004 season on such a high. But, for me, watching replays of the games and thinking back to my days as an All Black and living in New Zealand have given me my first spasms of homesickness. I wasn't expecting life in France to be a bed of roses. In fact, I'm not too sure what I was expecting. But when I think back to the comfortable familiarity of my former life and compare it to my new life here in France, I get these huge pangs of 'Oh my goodness, what the hell have I done?'

The reality of living in a foreign country is way different to the dreams I've had about it. There's no denying the culture here is taking some getting used to and the differences between New Zealand and

French rugby are huge. Nothing is like what I was used to — from the playing side to the medical, physio, rehab and administration. Life does not have the sheen I'd anticipated when the notion of living in France was nothing more than an idea — a good one too it seemed. Moving to France was going to give me a way to keep playing the game I love without the risks of burnout, being dropped and/or losing income and having the huge plus of being able to spend more time with my family. But despite my misgivings, I know all the above are still the right reasons for coming here and common sense tells me that time will make things better.

I am probably suffering from nothing more serious than a case of the mid-winter blues. Apparently when summer arrives we can expect to see fields of sunflowers stretching in every direction on the outskirts of the town, vineyards in full leaf too, and all of this under blue skies and temperatures of about 40 degrees. It's a scene that's hard to picture at the moment when it is more like –6°C.

I am constantly grateful to be living in a centrally heated and double-glazed house. Juanita keeps it at a toasty 20°C, which means there is no cold room anywhere in the house and doors can be left open without anyone yelling, 'Were you born in a tent!' The only downside is that you're never quite sure what it's actually like temperature-wise outside until you step outdoors. Sometimes, the difference can be quite pronounced!

Le tatouage. Tattoos. Despite the difficulties associated with language and culture, on and off the rugby pitch, my team-mates are a good bunch. The French guys in the team are especially keen to accentuate their individuality and several of them sport the rudest haircuts I have ever seen. I may never be renowned for following or creating fashion trends with my haircuts but I am pretty well known for my tattoos.

There were some pretty amazed stares in the Castres changing rooms early on and my tattoos proved to be a welcome ice-breaker. Quite a few of my team-mates have tattoos and they were quick to show me theirs, keen to let me know that we are one, so to speak, and convinced that their tattoos, like mine, are representative of Maori. But theirs are not Maori. They are simply some tattoo artist's interpretation of Maori.

When I was growing up and if you were tattooed as I am, you would automatically be typecast as a gang member. Part of the reason I wear all this moko is because I've become something of a role model and I want to help to get rid of the stigma that moko means bad things. It doesn't.

Back in the old days, moko was worn only by chiefs or important warriors, people of considerable status in their village or the tribe. Fast-forward to the 1970s and 80s and tattooing is associated with being a gang member. Fortunately, we've done a complete about turn now. The stigma is gone and it is socially acceptable to wear moko.

My mate Inia Taylor of Moko Ink, based in the Auckland suburb of Grey Lynn, has done all my more recent work. His clientele is a diverse mix of businesspeople and students, people from all walks of life.

But Inia refuses to tattoo gang members. That's one of his policies. He doesn't believe gang members have the right to wear it because they don't represent the people he wants to be wearing it — people who are looked up to, who have the mana to wear it and who are worthwhile disciples for this renaissance of ta moko — the art of tattooing. He's pretty staunch about that. Inia's made just a couple of exceptions and that is for the movie industry. He's done tattooing for *Once Were Warriors* and *What Becomes of the Broken Hearted?*.

When Inia started out he was one of few doing moko and he was often criticised by Maori for his tattooing of non-Maori. But his reasoning was that if you want worldwide recognition for Maori art, you can't limit yourself to allowing only Maori to wear it. Practically speaking, your stage would be too small.

Inia's got people wearing his work from UB40 to musician Michael Franti. Singer Robbie Williams was tattooed by one of Inia's friends. What better way to get Maoridom out to the world than have a superstar like Williams wearing the work? It has definitely raised the awareness of Maori art. These people respect what Maori are doing, they respect the trials and tribulations Maori have had to endure and that they are now standing up on their own two feet and being proud to be Maori.

Over the years, I think views have changed towards foreigners wearing moko. Its popularity means it is creating more work for Maori who may otherwise be on the dole. Where there used to be only two or three guys who did moko, now, up and down the country you've got more than 50. People travel to New Zealand so they can get a tattoo from a Maori.

I designed my first piece when I was an art student. I was 18 years old when I got it done. Note I said 'it'. At that stage is was just the one piece. A lot of the mates I grew up with were Polynesian and I wanted something that represented them as well as myself. I decided to get a *golima*, Samoan for arm band, which wasn't that common back then.

I thought getting the tattoo would hurt like hell but the actual process wasn't too bad. The guys who were doing it were saying to me, 'It's going to hurt on the inside of your arm.' But I was pretty

A New Year

relaxed about it all and when it was all over I left the place thinking, 'Hey, this still hasn't really hurt.' But a while later, yeah . . . !

Five years later I got my full arm done. It took about seven hours to complete. It is a representation of what I want to depict in terms of where I come from. Mania's close by the sea, the food source is the sea and the mountains. I used a couple of Samoan designs and the kowhaiwhai pattern to depict the mountains and the waves. The top and bottom parts were additions to the original I'd had done to mark the birth of my first son, Javier. It was finished the day after he was born. Then, when I was down in Otago in 1996, I extended it a bit, got two more, and they were to represent where I'd come to in myself. There's enjoyment here: pig tusks because I was really into pig hunting, and around the back there's a rugby ball, the top of it with the laces. There is a twin-band extension to represent my twins, Cayne and Tayla, so that to look at it now you can distinguish the three *golima* that represent my three older children. I thought I was going to stop there, but . . .

When Juanita and I got married we spent our honeymoon in Rarotonga. I wanted to get a tattoo over there, a piece of art that represents my self-exploration of being Maori. But then I decided, let's take this piece back even further to where Maori come from, which was Rarotonga and the Pacific triangle. So I got a triangular shape on the right side of my chest done to represent the Pacific triangle and seven waka along my collarbone, symbolising the large waka that basically populated the Pacific triangle. And I wanted some Tongan-Samoan designs to represent Juanita who is of Tongan-Samoan and Maori descent. Getting that tattoo took eight hours and it was done in one unforgettable stretch! I'd booked in with this guy thinking I had two days before we flew out but when I looked at our tickets I saw that we were actually flying out at five o'clock the following morning. When I turned up for my appointment I said, 'Come on mate, I'll make it worth your while.' I have to say there were times during the next eight hours when I was regretting my decision. I am sure he was working with blunt needles. It was probably the most painful tattooing I've ever had done.

I thought I would stop there. But then I decided I wanted just *one* more piece done — a shoulder and arm moko. Enter Inia. I'd heard about him through a friend of a friend. I started hanging out with him and we quickly discovered we had a lot in common. Inia showed me a few things he'd done, and he took photos of me and drew up a few examples. I liked what I saw. It was obvious to me that as we'd been talking he'd really listened to what I'd been saying, sussing out my view on things and what I thought was important. I was impressed. That's when I decided, let's do it, let's really make a piece of it.

The arm piece I'd gone to him about turned out to be the last thing he's done on me. By then it had gone from being just on the arm to 'let's do the shoulders and down the back a bit and then do the arm to finish it off'. At that stage, I hadn't ever considered getting my entire chest done.

Am I done yet? Probably not. I think of my moko as a work in progress and there are a few more things to add before it is complete. For me, moko is a deeply personal thing. What's it about? It's about me and I have made the choice to wear my life story on my body. If you like it, sweet. If you don't . . . so be it.

Above: Guess who? Me with Kevin Mealamu (seated), Carlos Spencer and Justin 'Gus' Collins on the night of my 30th birthday. Juanita threw me a surprise party — it was one of the best nights of my life.

Below: One of the most amazing experiences of my rugby career was meeting Bishop Desmond Tutu and Nelson Mandela on a Tri-Nations tour to South Africa in 2004. Here I'm pictured with Tana Umaga and Desmond Tutu.

About to embark on a new life in France. My arrival at Toulouse Blagnac International Airport, November 2004.

Rue Victor Hugo. A typically French street in the town of Castres.

Above: It had been snowing for three days solid when we 'snapped' this photo of our front yard in Castres. Below: The French do the festive season very well. Place Jean Jaures in the town square is covered in fairy lights for *le Noël*.

Above: Stade Pierre Antoine, my home ground for the next few years. Rain, snow or shine, the crowd always turns up for a home game. Below: On the hunt with the 'musketeer'. Both of us in our hunting attire — me à la Kiwi and him in full French costume.

Above: Juanita seated on the walls of Santa Bárbara Castle, high above Alicante, Spain. Below: Brad Fleming and me in the streets of Barcelona, just one of the many road trips we've taken around these parts.

Scrum practice with what I call the steam engine scrum machine. The French love to scrum. This was a small session — only 30 scrums this day!

More gesticulating! Me telling teammates which directions and weak points would be best to attack when running this move.

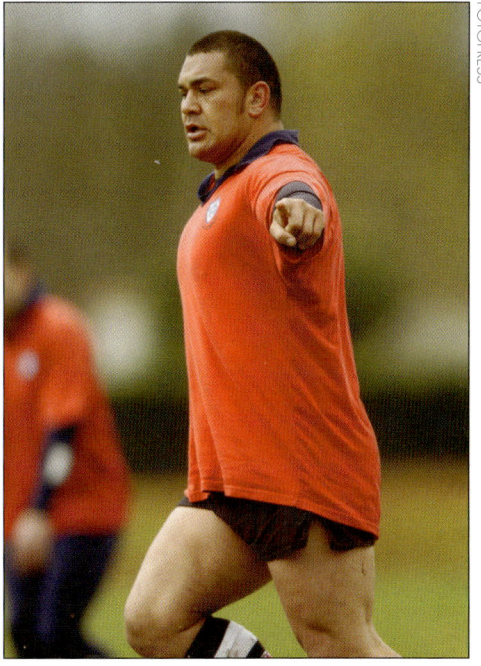

Me on defence — letting teammates know who I'm covering.

Typical Kees Meeuws 'pick 'n go' for my first try against Brive — I scored two in this game.

FOTOPRESS

9

Back to Work

Présent, mais ne pas corriger. Present, but not correct. With the new year well underway, I am keen to get back on the rugby field. Heineken Cup matches are finally over and the French championship once again kicks into gear. We have an away game against Bayonne, and to get there we go by bus. It's a four-and-a-half hour trip from Castres across to the south-western coast of France and uncharted territory for me.

The boys seem somewhat antsy on the coach trip but I am hopeful we can perform well while also getting those aggravating away-game blues out of our system. I'd like to think a win is possible, especially with the way the two teams stack up on the table. We are currently fourth and Bayonne lies well below us in 13th place. The teams last met back in August and during the second round, or *journée*, of this 2004–2005 championship. It was before my time here. It was a home game for Castres and therefore almost a given that we won. But judging by the scoreline of 36–32 it wasn't what you'd call a convincing win. But if you take the season since then, and given that there are only 16 teams in the competition, Castres is enjoying a much better run of form.

Certainly, luck seems to be on our side if you take our hotel into consideration. A 10-minute drive from the city of Bayonne, it's right on the beachfront looking out across the Bay of Biscay. The setting can only be described as beautiful. I go down to the water's edge and dare to dip my foot in the ocean. But I don't linger. It's a stormy day and I can only wonder at what it might be like here during summer months.

According to my reference books, Bayonne is an important port city. It is situated on the main route to Spain and straddles the rivers Adour and Nive. Like so many European settlements, it was founded by the Romans and has been ruled by both England and France. I was intrigued to learn that the bayonet, as used by the French army since 1703, originates from Bayonne.

But the region is probably better known, especially throughout Europe, for its summer resorts. I try to picture what the place must look like when the sun is shining and the beach crowded with bronzed, relaxed-looking holidaymakers. A lesser known fact is that Bayonne is also the home of a major European rehab centre to which sportspeople come to recuperate from injury. The list of elite athletes who have done time at the centre makes for impressive reading and includes the likes of soccer superstar Ronaldo.

Like so much of France, Bayonne has gained a reputation for goods you can either eat or drink: ham, Izarra liqueurs (a high-octane blend of Armagnac and alpine plants) and chocolates. It's the last item that intrigues me. I've discovered that Bayonne introduced chocolates to France. Astonishingly, at one time there were more chocolate artisans working in France than in Switzerland. And just in case you were in any doubt as to the importance of chocolate to the region, Bayonne plays host to a chocolate festival in early summer. It is definitely worth considering a return visit!

Un mauvais match. A bad game. Much to my dismay I discover that a new year does not herald a new era in Castres' rugby. Match day dawns bleak and unfortunately things only get worse. By the time the game kicks off the weather has gone from awful to completely atrocious and our play mirrors the conditions. Put bluntly, we play badly — exactly as we've trained all week. In the lead-up to this game, we hadn't practised our scrums because of injuries to players. And, on a personal note, the day before the game, I'm told I'll be playing loosehead. As preparation, it leaves a lot to be desired.

Despite our shoddy performance, the score is 12-all at halftime and it seems as though we are in with a chance. But my optimism is short-lived. Bayonne score a try soon after play resumes and our guys lose heart. It's like, 'Hey, it's just another away game after all' and I find the attitude hard to take.

Adding to our miserable performance, two of our players receive yellow cards, one in either half. On the other hand, Bayonne, who should be at a disadvantage when three of their team are sinbinned during the second half, somehow manage to score two converted tries on their way to what is a deserved 29–18 victory.

I'm furious and frustrated. It's yet another game in which we've failed to score tries, all our 18 points coming from the fortunately reliable boot of Richard Dourthe. The result sees us slip to sixth on the league table and Bayonne bounce up three places to 10th. I am far from happy with our level of performance and worry about our apparent inability to score tries.

Les Basques. Needless to say, I am not expecting to enjoy the after-match function but I can't help but be intrigued by the locals because they are so markedly different to the people from Castres. They even speak another language. We are most definitely in Basque country, home to explorers, philosophers and writers, artists, historians, political and religious leaders, and sportsmen and women. Golfer José María Olazabal is a Basque, as is tennis player Nathalie Tauziat. Famous cyclist Miguel Indurain is also from the region.

The Basque Country extends from Bayonne to Bilbao in Spain, a distance of about 100 km, and then inland 50 km. Apparently, the language of Basque, or Euskara, is spoken by about 660,000 people, less than 80,000 of whom live in France.

Think Basques, and it's almost automatic to think of ETA, the group that was founded in the early 1950s and originally called EKIN. Apparently ETA's *raison d'être* was to try to bring about the restoration of democracy to its regions — peacefully. But history shows that there was nothing amicable about the way democracy was originally wrenched from the Basques. Their rights were first taken during the bloody French Revolution and then further eroded by successive Spanish governments and the brutal regime of the fascist General Franco. During Franco's reign, Basque soldiers and politicians met fates of various kinds, anything from imprisonment and torture to death by the bullet. It was illegal to put a public face on being Basque or to speak the language.

It seems there is much that both sides have to be ashamed of

Back to Work

— tortures and murders, the 'death squads' of off-duty policemen, and the modern-day bombings of tourist resorts by ETA; these acts of terrorism are carried out by hard-core extremists who are demanding complete independence for the Basque Country.

It is, therefore, maybe an understatement to label them as simply a 'passionate people'. Their devotion to their heritage is tangible, even at a rugby club after-match function. The atmosphere is quite unlike anything I have experienced elsewhere in France and I am keen to learn more about these people and this region.

Joyeux anniversaire. Happy birthday. Inez turned one year old the day we played Bayonne, and now that I am back home we plan to celebrate her first year with a typically grand *soirée*, as is the tradition in our family. We invite some of my team-mates and French friends to a buffet brunch. It's a fairly international gathering, Juanita has been cooking for hours and we have 30-odd people due to arrive early afternoon.

The theme is fancy dress and soon our house is full of little fairies and various animals, a couple of Spidermen and a recognisable Snow White. Our two spare downstairs rooms house a playhouse and a bouncy castle (many thanks to Father Christmas and grandparents who love to spoil our girls). It's another great occasion of people, wine, food, music and conversation and the hours simply speed by. Next thing I know, it's midnight and Monday. My working week is about to begin and I only have time for a quick nap before training.

Une surprise méchante. A nasty surprise. At training I am told to take myself off to Toulouse for a VO2 max fitness test. Another of my team-mates, who was last seen enjoying himself at my place the previous evening, is commanded to take the test as well. Already dehydrated and hung over, we can now add stressed-out to our list of complaints!

It's not as if I've been going out of my way to be irresponsible either. Last Saturday we were told today would be about having a couple of scans and a blood test, and that's why I was pretty relaxed about having a few beers and wines at Inez's birthday party. Now, I'm anything but calm. I scull back water in an effort to hydrate and hope fervently that everything will turn out okay. I wonder what my blood pressure reading is right now.

Fortunately, the test is not until this afternoon and my teammate and I have a few hours to recover. But we aren't in a positive mood as we make the trip to Toulouse and all we manage to do is psyche each other out. Failure seems imminent. We try to push our fears to the back of our minds and decide the only solution is to give the test our best shot.

Upon arriving at the test centre, we are required to provide a urine sample (not hard to do given the amount of water we've been drinking), and have our skin folds measured (to determine body fat percentage). Blood is taken and we are given an ECG. Then it's a matter of getting all wired up for the run on the high-tech treadmill. Contrary to what I've been anticipating the test is not too bad and the results show I am fitter than I realised. In fact I am one of the fittest in the squad. Maybe, just maybe, wine really is the nectar of the gods!

Refroidi à l'os. Chilled to the bone. It's the last weekend in January and our weather has become an icy cocktail of snow and freezing temperatures. All week I've been training in snow, and I speak with some authority when I say that my extremities have never been so cold! The grounds are frozen and at trainings it feels as though we are running on concrete. We've been half-expecting today's game against Grenoble to be postponed, especially after the huge snowfall of just 48 hours ago. As I look out the window first thing I see it is still snowing.

However, the army comes to our rescue. During the morning, they shovel the snow from the pitch and, amazingly, especially in the eyes of a North Island Kiwi, conditions underfoot are perfect. I learn later that if the snow had been removed any earlier the ground would have had time to freeze over, thus making it impossible for the match to proceed.

As a setting for a game, it is picture perfect. The white snow is mounded thigh-high around the pitch which presents a perfect backdrop to the locals who turn out in their colourful droves to support the team.

It's a big day for me because it's the first time Juanita will see me play since she arrived in France. Despite our last woeful performance against Bayonne I am confident about today's game. If you work on the French theory, we should beat Grenoble, if only because it is our home game. Perhaps, more to our advantage, is the fact that prior to the start of the match our opposition is one of the three teams stuck in the championship's relegation zone.

Today we start well and are 13 points up after 20 minutes thanks to a penalty try, a conversion and two penalty goals from, you guessed it . . . Richard Dourthe. But then Grenoble claw back six points with two successful penalties.

As so often happens in games here, tempers flare and the tighthead props (I'm still playing at loosehead) from both sides are red-carded. The same incident also earns one of the Grenoble locks 10 minutes in the sin bin. Fortunately, we are able to make the most of our numbers advantage and score another converted try just before halftime.

Ten minutes into the second spell I score my first try, *un essai*, for Castres. It's the result of an all-forward effort. From a lineout, a ruck develops which becomes a driving maul. I am at the back and pretty much in the right place at the right time to get my hands on the ball and drive through to the line to score. As I run back to halfway I accept the pats on the back from my team-mates and acknowledge to myself how good it feels to have finally notched up a try for the team. And, remember, as the record holder for props scoring tries in test matches I have a reputation to maintain! Richard adds the conversion and we move ahead 27–9. It's a comfortable lead and it's great to be giving the local rugby fans plenty to cheer about.

However, the applause only seems to fire up Grenoble because they respond with two penalty goals. But back we come again with 20 minutes to go thanks to a try by our second-five Laurent Marticorena. Reliable Richard adds yet another conversion.

Although we let Grenoble in for a try six minutes later it never feels as though we're in danger of losing our grip on this game. But, it pays never to be complacent. Grenoble is determined not to make this game easy for us and the contest is more than just a little willing. With 10 minutes left on the clock, both teams have a player yellow-carded. I'm beginning to wonder if we will ever get through 80 minutes of rugby during this season with 15 players on the field.

But the scoring continues and we notch up another converted try due to the combined efforts of Romain Froment and, of course, Richard. And although Grenoble have the last say when their fullback scores minutes from the final whistle we get to walk off the pitch as winners by 41–22 and I think we can be justifiably pleased with our performance. Nothing beats the feeling of knowing you've had a good day at the office.

After the game I continue to be on a winner. It's an opportunity to catch up with my good mate John Blaikie. JB and I played six years of rugby together with Otago. Today he's been sidelined because of injury but it's great to be able to get together and compare notes on life in France.

Des moments de grand tension. Times of stress. Just days after the match against Grenoble we receive the news that not all our coaching panel have had their contracts renewed for the next season. Everyone is anxious and there is much speculation as to who will take over. It doesn't take long to find out what is happening: a case of coaching musical chairs. Bourgoin coach Laurent Seigne has been appointed as head coach of Castres for the 2005–2006 season and our forwards coach Christophe Urios is to move to Bourgoin. Meanwhile, our head coach Christian Gajan is set to travel much further afield. He's off to Japan to take up a coaching post with club Sunnix. Only backs coach Philippe Berot will remain at Castres.

Adding fuel to the already simmering fire, 16 players are also coming off contract. Grudges suddenly become obvious, as are the cliques that have developed within the team. Matters escalate bigtime during trainings. Fights break out, even to the extent that best friends start attacking one another. On one occasion it seems as though we are spectators to a farce — French-style of course. After a drill, one of our guys suddenly takes offence at his best mate's technique. Instead of both players just walking away, a few heated words are exchanged and suddenly one 'friend' is laying into the other and smacking him in the nose. The guy who takes one in the face turns and starts to walk off the pitch but then . . . whoa! He realises he is bleeding. Does he keep going? No way. Remember, this is France. He turns back and races over to his, for now, former friend and launches into him. It's like watching a human cockfight, and from where I'm standing it's one of the funniest things I've seen in a while. If you wanted to set the scene to music, the signature tune of *The Benny Hill Show* would be perfect.

Other members of the team attempt to separate the two but that doesn't stop the bloke with the bloodied nose from trying to sneak pot shots at his mate. Sensibly, the coaches call time on the training session, no doubt hoping that the tempers will cool as quickly as they were inflamed.

Although as a group who *do* control our tempers, it's the native English speakers who seem to be copping most of the flak within the squad. There is open resentment at the fact we tend to stick together as a group, at rugby and socially. To be frank, it's just our way of coping with the language barrier. Clearly, because of our limited French speaking and comprehension skills we are always the last ones to know what is going on.

But, in our defence, we're not the only ones to stick together. The guys who speak only French hang out as a group, as do those who are bilingual. Then there are the Spanish speakers. They too have formed their own little clique. I don't regard the situation as particularly unhealthy or abnormal, but because of the stress due to the imminent changes to both coaching staff and players, everyone is looking for someone or something to blame. Cultural and language differences seem to have become easy targets.

Back to Work

J'ai le mot sur (le bout de) la langue . . . je pense. The word is on the tip of my tongue . . . I think. It's not proving quite as easy to learn a new language as I thought it would be, although I'm picking up new words all the time and can converse with most people most of the time. But there's a world of difference between being able to make yourself understood and saying what you want how you want, to be able to gabble away in French with the same ease with which I speak English and to have what I'd consider a normal conversation. No searching for words, no big pauses or stopping to mentally translate from French to English what has been said and then working out my response, thinking it through in English and then finding the appropriate words or French phrases.

The frustrations come when I can't say what I really want to say, and that I don't as yet possess the verbal artillery to get me straight to a point. It means I have to take the long way round. If I don't know the word I resort to pointing or waving my hands around in that time-honoured French tradition. Or, when none of the above works, I have to grab someone who can speak English and French to translate for me.

Unfortunately, because of our training schedule and other obligations to the club, I've only been able to fit in two lessons since I've been here. We've bought heaps of textbooks and I've found another novel way to do my 'homework'. As part of the Sky network we can watch the French TV channel *Canal Plus*. It's proving really helpful because I can watch a movie with subtitles and listen to the English words while reading the French translation.

Like a lot of foreigners, I'm finding it easier to understand conversation than to speak, especially if people speak slowly. The hardest part is when they speak as they normally would and then, to me, an entire sentence can sound like one rather long word. It's definitely a confidence thing — and of course I speak fluent (or should that be fluid) French when I've enjoyed a few drinks!

It's certainly to my advantage that I don't mind making mistakes. Sometimes I'll say a word and the person I'm talking to will look at me in such a way that I know I haven't got it right. So then I'll have another try and they generally cotton on to what it is I'm trying to say, correct my attempts, give me an answer, I'll say '*Merci*' and we're all happy.

The physio here, Olivier Marty, has been helping me out a lot. Right from the start he's been very encouraging and telling me I'm doing really well. His support has been a big confidence booster for me. Whenever I go to see him we speak a mixture of part-English, part-French. For example, he might ask me what my cellphone number is in French. Simple, I hear you sniggering! Believe me, understanding the French system of numbers can take some getting to grips with. Olivier explained that French and Spanish are the only languages that count up to 60, *soixante*, and then go to 60-plus as in *soixante-dix* which is 70 (60 plus 10) until you get up to 80, *quatre-vingt* (four 20s). From then on it becomes four times 20 plus one, two, three and so on. If you ask me, it seems like a really weird way to count up to 100. But once you get the hang of it, it's all quite easy.

On the rugby pitch, I don't really have any problems understanding what's going on and as my team-mates' accents become more familiar I am becoming increasingly confident. I know the lineout calls. They're numbers, which is probably the main reason I've been able to pick up the French way of numbers pretty quick, and apart from that all I'm looking for is where the ball is going and what move the backs are planning on doing. Also, I now have a better idea of what the game plan is all about, and if all else fails there are four or five other English-speaking guys in the team who can help put me straight.

My French accent might need a little work but it's my English-when-speaking-to-a-French-person voice that has Juanita in stitches. I've fallen into the habit of speaking English with a distinctive French accent, reminiscent of *'Allo, 'Allo* perhaps. Apparently I also speak English with an Argentinean twist when speaking to my South American team-mates. But I get pulled up at home when I break into pidgin English.

It might sound strange, but when I'm talking with people who have learned English as their second or third language, it makes me easier for them to understand if I imitate their accents, and it's certainly helped our team-mates' level of communication. I'm all about pidgin English these days, bro!

Revenons à ce qui nous préoccupé. Let's get back to the point. Rugby is what we, as a group of guys, are here for and it's important the team comes together, that we manage to put our differences and concerns aside and concentrate on our next goal, which is to beat Béziers away from home.

Given our poor on-the-road record I can't say I'm totally confident of victory despite the fact Béziers is hovering near the bottom of the table, and that in the previous round the side had taken a severe beating from Toulouse, losing 46–10.

On the plus side, we work well in our training sessions in the lead-up to the match. Our forward pack has something to prove and that fact concentrates the minds. Béziers has a huge scrum and it's about the only area of their game in which they have been destroying other teams. This is not good news for us because our scrum has been a bit shaky of late, something I put down to the stresses we have been under. Also, we're short of a lock. But the good news is that our big No 8, Rodrigo Capo Ortega, is back in the starting lineup after being sidelined due to an 'attitude problem'. Apparently during this season's first-round match against Grenoble, he'd been KO'd by one of the opposition players. Being a fiery Uruguayan, he came to declaring war on the player and stating he was going 'to kill him' when the teams met again in the return match. Our coaches obviously decided Rodrigo is quite mad enough to attempt to carry out his threat so it was positive intervention on their part that saw him sit out the game against Grenoble.

Meanwhile, I'm still struggling slightly with my hamstring injury and the decision is made to bring me on as an impact player.

We get off to a bad start. Béziers score a converted try just three minutes into the game. But once again Richard Dourthe keeps us in the game and his three successful shots at goal in the space of five minutes put us ahead. But the lead changes hands when the Béziers' kicker raises the flags twice during the second quarter. But we don't allow them to get out of sight and at halftime we're trailing by just four points.

The real positive is that our scrum is more than holding its own and as the game wears on we begin to dominate that all-important aspect of the game. Placed under pressure, Béziers start to crack. The kickers from both sides land another two successful penalty goals each, but Richard finishes with a flourish, landing three from three attempts to give him a 100 per cent kicking record for the match and, finally, Castres notches up a vitally important 24–19 win away from home. Suddenly, we're all friends again. The coaches are happy and the team settles down.

It's a huge relief all round. Next weekend there is no club rugby because of the Six Nations tournament and my family and I have planned a trip away. Barcelona, home of the Picasso Museum, here we come! We know we'll enjoy ourselves much more if we don't have to worry about team antics.

10

Art

Ma passion: art. My passion: art. It's easy to make sweeping generalisations of what people may or may not be, and goodness knows I've been on the receiving end of a fair few wildly inaccurate statements over the years. Kees Meeuws is well-built and that means he must be taking steroids. A Maori and sporting a few tattoos? Tick the wife-beater box. Of course, I'm a front-row forward and that means I have a distinct lack of both brain power and imagination. But an artist? You've got to be joking mate! Kees Meeuws? An artist? Yes ladies and gentlemen, an artist, and extremely proud to be so.

I've always loved making things. Building blocks were my first medium of choice. Our family had truckloads of Lego and Duplo and my younger brother and I would spend many happy evening hours with our blocks, creating constructions where imagination was our only limiting factor. And fortunately we both had plenty of that.

Le Rugbyman

Good with my hands, I was always into art of some sort, drawing or making things, imitating my father who was a master of tinkering and never happier than when he was working on some project or other in the garage of the house he'd built with his own hands.

Early on, my artistic bent was satisfied with the drawing of planes, battleships and cars. As I got older I moved on to more animate objects such as toys, bows and arrows and guns. Trolleys were the big go during my intermediate school years. They were the perfect mode of transport for outdoorsy 11- and 12-year-old types. Because we lived on a bit of a hill a whole range of possibilities opened up to us, from the actual construction stages to the tweaking around to make our trolleys go faster and look better. Due to the racing there were also endless occasions when we would need to repair our vehicles and, of course, who could resist having just another dabble? Surely there must be a way to get just a *little* more speed out of those trolleys! Building huts was another favourite pastime, another way in which we could indulge our creative desires. Close by where we lived there were a lot of reserves and they were perfect places to play in and to do a little building work.

It takes special people to recognise and nurture talent and I was very fortunate to have the encouragement of a number of teachers. It was Mrs Kennedy who ignited the artistic fire in me when I was a pupil at Rangeview Intermediate School. I will always be grateful to her for her guidance.

At high school, it was more of the same. Fortunately, that I was a rugby player of some skill did not dissuade my art teachers from urging me to continue to develop my talents. Although a lot of people think rugby and art are a strange mix to find in one person, I, and obviously my teachers, never doubted that in my case the two such different fields could co-exist quite happily.

Art

From my own point of view, I don't see why rugby and art should be looked upon as any more strange a combination than rugby and commerce. There are plenty of accountants out there playing rugby after all.

I had some really good art teachers at Kelston Boys High. The artist and sculptor Simon Johnson taught me all about sculpture, and Kit McIntyre was my painting tutor. Kit hails from Ireland and she arrived at the school during my fifth form year. She was awesome, of great value to me, and she taught me a hell of a lot about the dynamics of paintings, about painting and the way to approach art.

In my seventh form year the school's art department was enlarged and a new facility built, which meant the school could employ a teacher of sculpture. Enter Simon Johnson. He'd done his degree at Auckland's Elam School of Fine Arts and was straight out of training college. Incredibly enthusiastic, Simon and I related really well and he pretty much ignited my passion for sculpture. It was during that year I had to make a decision about my future and he pushed me to apply to all the art schools.

At that stage my first choice was to go the AUT School of Design. I had my heart set on a career as a graphic artist. But AUT turned me down. I was quite peeved, disappointed to have been rejected and also unsure of what to do next. But fortunately, thanks to Simon's insistence, I'd also applied to Elam. They accepted me.

I was pretty stoked to win a place at the college and I just loved my first year there. It was like an induction course and we had the opportunity to work in a variety of media. But sculpture was where I wanted to be and the following year I selected it as my major.

But I didn't finish the year out or get to complete my degree.

Le Rugbyman

My father died and with it went my will to continue my studies. Dad's death was a difficult time in my life. I was just 20 years old and now I'd lost both my parents. It was quite one thing to cope with the loss of my father but, suddenly, my art, that creative instinct that had always been such a vital part of me, was also gone. Looking back, it's like I suffered a mental block. Art wasn't right for me at that time but rugby was. I was given the opportunity to move to Dunedin to play and that's what I did.

Sculpture is where I want to go to next in my life. It will be the medium I follow when I've finished playing rugby. I'm not expecting the road to be easy, in fact it could get quite rocky, but it's important to me that at some time in the future I get back on track. It may turn out that I don't pick up exactly where I left off, although I am quite keen to go back to Elam and finish off my degree.

I tried to do it in 2003 when I was playing for the Blues, but because art is so practical you have to be able to attend lectures all the time. Unfortunately, because of my rugby commitments there was no way I could attend all the lectures, let alone keep up with the requirements of the course to finish my degree. So, once again I've put it on hold but I still regard it as a very real option for me when I stop playing rugby. Sure, I'll be an old bugger by then but I reckon I'll still be keen to give it a go.

C'est là, dans ma tête. It's there, in my head. To sculpt you require vision, the ability to be able to see the end product. If your mind is unable to create something from nothing, that's what you will end up with — nothing. If, for example, you're carving from a block of wood, you have to see in the wood what you want out of it. Most people get their ideas through the drawing and developing of their

Art

ideas and then by the actual making of it, thinking, 'Okay, that doesn't look right but we'll go on and try this . . . '

I'm more inclined to work the other way round, however. Give me a bit of wood or rock, and if I've got an idea in my head I'll have a crack at how I want it to go, and if it doesn't work out I'll move on to the next one. That's the way I do things and how I learn.

Suffice to say, I wasn't big on the workbooks at art school. After I'd created the pieces I'd then have to go back and do the development pictures, all the things I was supposed to have done first. My art teachers used to crack up at me. They'd see my finished work and ask me how I got there. I'd be pointing to my head and saying, 'It's all up in here, that's the way I work,' and then they'd come back with, 'Look mate, this is what is expected from you at art school.' *That's* when I'd have to go back and do all the working drawings.

I know it's not the way for everyone, but once the piece is created in my head and I've worked out how I'm going to achieve it, I like to get stuck in. Back in New Zealand, Juanita might be dragging me out of the garage in the wee small hours. But that's the way I am when I get into something, I immerse myself in it and I'll happily work away until about 3 am or later to get finished.

The latest thing I made was a knife and handle, the blade from paua shell and the handle from native rimu, to cut the umbilical cord when Inez was born, a mata iho which translates literally as mata, blade, and iho, umbilical cord. For me, it's quite a significant thing to do, following the traditions of Maori and Pacific Islanders who used shell to cut the cord. Hence my decision to use paua shell and to opt for a native timber handle.

I started with a big piece of wood, then cut it down to the size I wanted and drew out the shape. The last one I'd made, for when Eva was born, was the first carving I'd ever really done and the handle on that one was quite straight. I was never completely satisfied with it — the big curve of the blade and the straight handle — so when I was doing the one for Inez I thought, 'Okay, it's got this curve so I'll try to make the handle a curve too just to balance it up.'

That's how I develop my art pieces, by not being completely happy with them and then refining my technique or ideas, doing them over and over until they are where I want them to be. I'm sure that should we have another baby the mata iho I carve will be totally different from the ones I've already made.

Do I have influences? My major ones are simply a combination of my experiences and what I'm carving at the time. I'm really into incorporating man-made materials with natural materials. I like using steel and wood, glass and wood, things that have both natural and man-made components. Also, it's about the two worlds we live in, the natural and the manufactured, either side by side or somehow integrated. It's where I approach my work from.

Prior to focusing on contemporary Maori art, I was into a lot of stuff such as Claes Oldenburg's work. He's a Swedish-born American artist who takes functional objects and make sculptures out of them using non-functional materials. As an example, he made a wash basin out of PVC. You could see very clearly what it was meant to be — it even had taps attached to it — but because it was drooping off the wall it was unusable. I like the concept of grabbing everyday items, the things we take for granted, and making them out of another material, of coming up with a work that makes you stop and think.

I once made a massive razor out of wood. It was about six feet tall. People would come in and say, 'Oh shit, a six-foot tall razor!

Art

What was he thinking about when he was doing that?' That's the sort of thing I plan on doing, definitely: making the extraordinary out of the ordinary. I like that it makes people think.

Do I have a definition of art? I think it's all in the eye of the beholder. You get from art what you see and how you see, and if you enjoy it, that's good. If it makes you think, even better, but if you don't enjoy it, that's also part of it. Someone else will.

If people are interested in it and they call it art, then it is art — to them. It's the same as if something some regard as art is looked on as nothing more than a piece of garbage to others.

Art is extremely personal. I guess that as an artist, it pays not be too precious, too thin-skinned. My career as a rugby player is certainly providing me with the perfect education on how to accept criticism!

Personally, I think art should speak for itself. There shouldn't need to be a written explanation by the artist as to what their art is about and the reasoning for it. I think too many artists are letting their words, their original literature, do the speaking for their art. Instead, they should let their art do the talking.

That's one of the reasons why I admire Ralph Hotere. He lets his art do the talking. There are all these people out there writing about why he's done things, and it cracks me up. I guess people like to think they're an authority on his work and what it means but maybe they've got it completely wrong and what they say is not what he was thinking of at all. Sure, you can probably try to guess at what he's thinking, but you can never know for sure. I wonder if some day people are going to be writing about my art in a rather pretentious way and trying to tell me, along with everyone else, what I was thinking at the time I created it.

Coming to France is partly about my wish to develop my art. It's all part of my game plan for life. In the grand scheme of things, by playing rugby here for a few years I hope to have enough money put aside so I can then either go back to school and finish my degree or just get in there, get my hands dirty and try to sculpt. I want to spend more time on my art but to date I haven't had the luxury of the quality time that I need to develop my ideas.

I guess most people would consider a career as an artist to be even more tenuous than that of a professional rugby player. But I want to give it a go. I regard art as my true calling. I have faith in my own ability and it will be interesting to see if I can make a name for myself in another field. I remain hopeful.

Émerveillé. (Lost) in wonder. Wow! From where I'm standing my rugby career has never looked so good. A mere three-and-a-half hours' drive along excellent highways and I'm standing in the centre of Barcelona. I am captivated. What a fantastic-looking place and it only gets better the more I explore. Art in some form or other adorns the skyline, the city parks and just about any space you care to think of — from roundabouts to jetties. If there's potential to have an empty space, the Spanish fill it with art. How wonderful.

Brad and Adele are with us. We travelled separately but in convoy, and together we trawl the streets and the museums. Nothing or no one is going to stop me from visiting the Picasso Museum. Picasso is among my favourite artists. He spent a great deal of his life based in Barcelona and the museum in his honour houses the most extensive collection of his works in the world.

I am thrilled to be able to see in person some of the most well-known works by one of the greatest artists this world has ever known, to be

Art

able to study in detail his styles and their development. For me, it's an amazing experience and I'd rate the museum as a 'must-see' for anyone planning a trip to Barcelona, and even for those who aren't big art fans.

Sightseeing is a must-do for our happy band of tourists. We manage a walk along the famous La Rambla, the most cosmopolitan street in Barcelona, and what a veritable melting pot of people walk along it. Everyone is here and I mean literally *everyone*, tourists of course but also locals out shopping, and businesspeople too, from the straight-up businessmen to the ladies who ply their trade, most often in the evenings. It's a fascinating and buzzing place.

In Arabic, *ramla* means torrent and this wide street, now divided into five continuous sections, used to be a small stream outside the city walls. Universities and convents were built on its banks during the 16th century, and 300 years later when the city walls were torn down buildings were constructed where the by-now dried up stream used to be. So maybe the *ramla* was more trickle than torrent all those centuries ago but now it more than lives up to its name — except there are humans surging down the street rather than water, wave after wave of people from all over the world. It feels great to be among them, to be just another tourist savouring the sights. Have I mentioned just how much I'm enjoying my life?

In order to see more of the city we take a bus tour. It's one of those where you can get on and off as you please. Our first point of disembarkation is the Sagrada Famillia Gaudi Cathedral. It's breathtaking. I've never seen anything like it. From the outside it looks like an enormous candle dripping wax. The architect was the eccentric Antoni Gaudi who dedicated the last 43 years of his life to its construction. He met a rather sad end when, as a 74 year old, he was run over by a tram. He is buried in the crypt.

Amazingly, the cathedral remains a work in progress. Started more than a century ago, it is predicted there are still decades more work involved before it will be completed. Donations from churchgoers and visitors help to keep the construction work going. We promise ourselves that we will have to keep returning here to check on progress.

Next up we plan to visit Parc Güell, the land and home of Gaudi up to the time he died. However, we take a brief time out from sightseeing because during the walk from the bus stop we feel a hunger coming on and we stop to sample some traditional Spanish cuisine at a café halfway up the hill. We choose the *paella*, a rice dish accompanied by all sorts of meats, fish and seafood. It's delicious, and with fuel on board we make it to the top of the hill without any problems. In the *parc* we find the longest park bench in the world. Serpentine-shaped and incorporating water fountains and alcoves, it is perched on the hillside and provides us with a good place to rest our weary feet while admiring the views of Barcelona.

Around us, all is wonderful and weird. Walls that look like natural caves in the terraced hillside are revealed under closer inspection to be man-made and the place is full of eccentric sculptures, including ones of giant ants crawling up the side of Gaudi's house. Then, strolling through the garden paths, we hear music. Buskers. It's almost magical, certainly ethereal, because just as you move out of earshot of one musician another takes over, the harmonies never jar and your walk becomes a relaxing meander — but one which left me skint of spare change!

As a weekend getaway it's fantastic. We vow to return because there is still so much to see and do and as we head back to Castres we're already looking forward to our next visit to the Catalunyan capital.

Art

La merde arrive. Shit happens. I'm injured! And, I'm furious! My hamstring injury has been misdiagnosed and in fact I've torn the muscle sheath from the muscle, plus torn my muscle. It looks as though I'm going to be out of action for three weeks but because of a mandatory holiday it will be five weeks before I get to pull on my boots to play again. I hate being injured and I'm beginning to feel aggravated with the way this season is going. Because I've been ineligible for the Heineken Cup it means I'm only getting my rugby in dribs and drabs. And now I'm facing another lengthy interruption that I really don't need. To compound matters, had the injury been properly diagnosed in the first place I wouldn't be in this position now.

This is my book and so I'm allowing myself one whinge! The medical staff at the club are nothing like the efficient and switched-on staff I'm used to back home. It's almost as if they are too scared to diagnose anything. In fact our physio isn't even employed on a fulltime basis.

Whenever an injury or a problem occurs the player is whisked off to Toulouse for a scan. This takes about two to three hours out of your day if you include the drive there and back, which all amounts to a significant waste of time, and trainings get missed as well. I'm starting to feel on the outer. Because I'm injured I no longer have the same contact with my team-mates and I'm constantly on the road travelling to Toulouse and back.

I'm even more pissed off because it was a radiographer in Toulouse who gave me the all-clear to keep playing when my leg wasn't right and which has resulted in my worsened injury. Yet a radiographer from Castres, who scanned my leg in the Castres hospital, could see the problem as plain as day.

Le Rugbyman

I'm beginning to feel like the guy who retires from international rugby and then only turns up to collect his pay cheque. This frustrates the hell out of me and even more so when I meet up with my team-mates and they start calling me Frank Bunce (sorry cuz)! Poor Frank was here for a season and busted his knee after one game. Rumour has it that he did his OE here instead. You can see the similarity, can't you? I've also had my fair share of traipsing all over the countryside — but *only* when the opportunity has presented itself of course. I hate not being able to play.

Sous la pression. Under pressure. For the next two weeks I can only sit on the sideline and watch my team play. We beat Auch 25–18 at home and then lose away to Perpignan 10–20. It's two nights before the big one against Bourgoin and things are getting desperate. Bourgoin are top of the table and Castres not only want a win, we are in dire need of one. But I am not the only injured prop. One of the others has a broken finger and popped ribs. There is no way he can take the field and we're going to have to play one of our looseheads at tighthead.

In the days leading up to the game I go out for a meal with a team-mate and his friends from the UK. I'm halfway through my meal of flounder, known here as *boubou*, when my cellphone rings. I miss the call. Within two minutes a waitress approaches the table with a portable phone and hands it to me. It's the club's general manager wanting to discuss my injury and to know whether there's any chance of me playing against Bourgoin.

I don't enjoy the conversation. My physio has told me that if I play too soon I'll be at risk of damaging myself so badly I'll be out for the rest of the season. He said the injury needs time to heal completely and two weeks off isn't going to cut it. Club management know what the situation is — they've spoken to the physio — and yet they still want to know how I'm feeling and if I think I can play. I know exactly how I'm feeling. Under pressure! It's crazy.

Later that night the head coach rings me to say the club president is coming to training in the morning to discuss the situation with me. He advises me not to train in the morning and to stick to my guns of not playing because he doesn't want to jeopardise my injury further. It's good to know I have his support, although it doesn't entirely ease that sick feeling I have in the pit of my stomach. The flounder is floundering!

However, *monsieur le president* never appears. The phone call from the club manager and a call to my physio convinced him I shouldn't play.

As it turns out, the team does well without me. The boys are fired up. Mauricio plays really well at tighthead and our scrum dominates. We win 31–29. It's a narrow victory but we'll take it. Afterwards, Mauricio comes up to me and tells me in his less than pidgin English that I can keep the tighthead spot. It wasn't for him. It's nice to know my position isn't under threat. But I hate not playing, and did I tell you . . . I hate being injured!

11
A Hunting We Will Go

La chasse. The hunt. Rugby might be my number-one sport but it's also my living. This means I have to find other ways to let off steam. Following another sport as a spectator is not really my thing — I'm most definitely an action man. When I want to get physical away from the rugby field you'll find me thrashing about in the wild chasing a four-legged beast. I'm a hunter, a pig hunter to be precise.

I can remember the first time I went hunting as if it were yesterday. I was 13 years old, it was Labour Weekend and a group of us from our street decided to head to Whitianga for the long weekend. It was there that I got my first taste of pig hunting and if you can refer to a sport in such terms, well . . . it was love at first sight. Everything about the experience appealed to me, no matter that the pig we caught was pretty much a tiddler: the way the dogs worked, watching them out-scent the pig and bailing it up until we reached them. Then there was the fun task of sticking the animal. Don't worry, it wasn't anything like playing out a *Lord of the Flies* scenario, but for a young Westie the experience stirred something primal in me — I am a hunter-gatherer-type persona.

Years down the track and as an adult, the sport's appeal to me lies largely in its challenges. Like rugby, the challenges of hunting are constant. You've got to take a considered approach. It can be quite dangerous: a pig can seriously rip you up or even kill you if it's big enough. But even more than the actual hunt, the testing times that come *after* what I regard as the easy parts — the hunting out and killing of the pig — are when I start to get excited. That's when the true test of character begins on both physical and mental levels — the carrying of the pig carcass back to the truck.

I look at it like this. If I go out on a pig hunt and don't catch anything, hey, I've been on a bush walk. But catch something and that's when the adrenaline kicks in for me because I know the real hard yards are about to begin. As soon as the dogs begin to bark I'm mentally preparing myself for the challenges that await me.

A pig can range in size from an 80-pounder to up around the 200-pound mark. When I go out with my mates in New Zealand, it falls mainly (and quite literally) on my shoulders to carry the carcass back to our vehicle. Sometimes I share the task, it depends on whom I'm with on the day, and as I'm generally one of the bigger blokes I'm more of a natural for the job. Plus, of course, I enjoy it. Sometimes I'll have to plot a course up a steep gully or over difficult terrain, but all the time I'm carrying what is literally a dead weight. It's not easy. In fact it can be bloody difficult.

It comes down to the absolute basics. One man against one animal; and there's no way I want a dead pig to beat me. Yet, it can often seem as if the advantage is with the animal because the man carrying the beast discovers that he is competing against himself. It's very easy to say, 'Yeah, I caught it,' and leave the beast there.

It's strange how you can be so challenged — mentally and physically taken to the very limits of your capabilities — and later be able to take the time to reflect that, actually, you've been put through a good learning curve. You're allowed to pat yourself on the back if you want to; after all, you've achieved your goal of getting a pig carcass back to a truck, and at times that objective, the truck deck, has seemed like an unattainable target. But once you get there, once you realise your goal and can appreciate how you coped with the sheer physicality and mental toughness, well, in my book you're setting yourself up to be able to achieve anything you want to do. It's the buzz you get from knowing you've been able to accomplish the task that gives you the confidence to try new things away from hunting. Or, that's the way it has worked for me.

It's all about being up to the task mentally. I think my pig hunting has held me in good stead throughout my test rugby career — and beyond. I know when times get tough I can push through them because that's what I'm used to doing — in my day job and in my chosen recreation.

With rugby, I'm doing it most weekends, walking up that metaphoric cliff face or down into a gully. Sometimes I'm on my own and sometimes I have my mates alongside, right there and willing to lend a hand when the going gets tough. Hunting is about being both an individual and a team player; it's about being able to lead from the front or being prepared to share the load. It's no different to performing on the rugby pitch where it's about doing the best you can do in your particular position and as part of a team, and also being able to inspire your team-mates to perform at their best.

I can't ever imagine not hunting. I plan to be doing it for the rest of my life. And I make no apologies for the fact that I'm a hunter-gatherer, a 'me-man, me-hunt' type of bloke. If times get tough, I like knowing I have the ability to put food on the table for my family. You know me! I'm into anything that has to do with food!

À la campagne. In the country. So you can imagine how excited I am when my new French friend Bruno Delpino invites me to go on a day's hunting trip. It's been far too long between hunts and I'm really keen to see how things are done in this part of the world. Plus, a day out in the bush is just what I need to clear my head, to stop me from worrying about my injury and my lack of game time or, at the very least, I hope it will help me to put my situation in perspective. Also, hunting provides me with a solid aerobic workout. As I get ready for my day out I envisage myself striding out over French mountainsides or straddling bluffs. I can hardly wait to get going.

I arrange to meet Bruno at his place. Ready for action and eager to get hands-on with our prey, I'm togged out in my typical Kiwi hunting gear of hunting trousers, boots, polar fleece and wet weather gear — and carrying my knives.

I do a bit of a double take when I see Bruno. He's dressed in very civilian attire, a polo shirt and jeans! Not hunting attire as I know it. I don't say anything and he makes no comment about my mode of dress either, so I decide he must have his hunting gear in a bag and will change into more suitable outdoor wear later on.

Before we head away we have a coffee and a chat and we're joined by two of Bruno's friends, also decked out in street-casual clothing.

A Hunting We Will Go

We're in the car and on our way before I notice that none of my travelling companions seems to have brought a change of clothes. Don't they know the first thing about hunting? I offer up a mental shrug. The French continue to bemuse me. But I feel justified in giving myself a pat on the back. At least one of us knows how to dress appropriately for a hunt.

Our drive takes us about half an hour east of Toulouse towards Bayonne until we reach our destination, Mauran, yet another beautiful French village. Bruno's friend, François, who looks like your typical French publican, stout and sporting a large bright-red proboscis, is there to greet us. In fact, you'd have to be blind to miss him. He is dressed in a knee-length black velvet jacket that is adorned with sparkling gold buttons. Under this he has on a rust-coloured waistcoat that covers most of what seems to be some sort of white frou-frou sleeved shirt. On his white cravat a hunting logo pin flashes in the sunlight. The bottom half of his outfit is just as amazing. Françoise is wearing neither jeans nor hunting trousers. Instead he has on riding pants, which are tucked neatly into his buttoned-up knee-high socks. It was only a short drive from Castres to Mauran but I feel as if I've travelled back in time — quite a long time really — more like centuries than decades, to suddenly find myself hooked up with one of the musketeers. I know I'm staring. Mind you, he's looking sideways at me too.

Monsieur le musketeer has driven here in a massive truck that houses a horse called Hercules. He suits his name because he's a huge beast. There are also 20-something dogs on board. Despite the dubious fashions on display, I'm encouraged. With this number of dogs we're bound to catch something. I ask what it is we're hunting because to date no one's actually mentioned what our quarry is.

Le Rugbyman

But suddenly more people arrive, including the village mayor (which brings our number of hunters up to a dozen) and I'm asked to help carry the barbecue-grill from the nearby clubhouse.

Although I'm raring to get going, I'm happy to wait a few minutes more. It seems a sensible idea to set out *le pique-nique* before we head away because we're bound to be ravenous after the hunt.

Wait a second, I've obviously misunderstood. No sooner are the food and cases of wine unloaded than I'm invited to sit down and join the feast. I try to hide my amazement. 'Hey everyone,' I feel like shouting, 'we haven't caught anything yet!'

But this is hunting French-style. I should have known it would involve food and drink. From what I can gather, hunting traditions in France dictate that we celebrate the hunt before it actually takes place. Needless to say there are copious amounts of wine consumed and all manner of French sausage, breads, cheeses, *pâtés* and hot meats to be enjoyed. By the time we finish eating I can't be fagged hunting, and in fact I feel more inclined to wander off and have a bit of a sleep.

However, it's not a good time to nod off because, finally, the hunt is about to start. A couple of guys dressed in musketeer-type attire, which makes them look like François' twin brothers, break out their brassware and start blowing what must be a French hunting tune. They then leap astride their horses and lead the dogs to the bottom of a hill to start the hunt. Meanwhile I find myself ushered into a car and driven to the top of a nearby hill.

It's a vastly different approach to hunting as I know it, not much leg-stretching and aerobic exercise here, but I can only guess we're going to where we can cut off the animal from above, the dogs leading the quarry up to the ridge where we're now standing.

A Hunting We Will Go

Standing! That's what I'm doing, not thrashing through the bush, scaling hillsides or clambering down gullies. I'm standing on a hilltop that is providing a group of gentlemen with a perfect vantage point from which to view a hunt. It's about now that realisation dawns. My invitation to this hunt only ever extended to me being a spectator. I suddenly feel quite the prize prick dressed as I am in my hunting gear. Thankfully, I've left my knives in the car.

There's nothing for it but to watch on politely from the sidelines as the dogs go about their business of chasing a deer. It's on the small side, hardly bigger than Bambi for goodness' sake and known locally as a white tail or barking deer. A bit like me, perhaps, barking mad to think I was going on a real hunt! And in a pig versus deer kai contest, it's well . . . no contest. I could polish off this deer in one sitting.

For three hours we stand on the hilltop and watch the dogs go through their paces. They don't seem particularly interested in the deer and are quite content to wander past it a few times, give it a bit of a sniff and continue on. We decide to call it a day.

Such is the nature of the beast: some days are good for hunting; others not so good. But one thing is for sure. A bad day out hunting still beats a good day at work.

12
Spring in the Air

La nourriture pour à pensé. Food for thought. Over the past few months our newfound French friends have introduced us to the many delights of French cuisine. Bruno is an exceptional cook and delights in giving us tours of his heritage, which is both Spanish and French, through food. In February, we were treated to a Spanish-themed dinner where we ate paella and drank Spanish wine. And now, with my mother-in-law Elaine in town, Bruno and Laurence decide to host a meal in her honour.

It's going to be a traditional Tarn meal (Castres is in the province of Tarn).

Comme d'habitude we start off with Tarn *foie gras* and sip on wine chosen especially to accompany this dish. *Magret du Canard* follows. This is duck breast grilled as you would a steak and served with potatoes and mushrooms. To wash this down we drink more wine

— representative of the region of course. The French always have dessert. Tonight it's a pine nut tart. Quite simply, it's delicious.

I really enjoy these meals. Whether they are long lunches or leisurely evening meals, they provide excellent opportunities for me to practise speaking French and to learn more about the culture and way of life we have chosen for ourselves.

With Eva at school and Juanita increasingly involved in various school activities, our network of French friends is widening and with it our social calendar is becoming busier. It's often said that the French are standoffish but our experiences disprove that theory. We find the people here warm, open and friendly, and just as eager to learn about our culture and country, and us as individuals, as we are about them. I also look forward to reciprocating their hospitality and am keen to show them the delights of Kiwi cuisine. I will need to stock up on certain items when I'm home next. I think the 'Kiwi Kai Cooker' will be top of my list. I've checked out the rocks here and they're not conducive to firing up for a hangi pit. I'm slowly perfecting my Maori strum too, in readiness for the guitar session that follows a feed.

Un carnaval. A carnival. It's a sweltering spring day, a far cry from a mere two weeks ago when each morning we were waking to temperatures of −10°C. This much more pleasant and hot weather makes it easy to get into party mood. Today is carnival day and our little schoolgirl Eva is about to be part of the parade, all dressed up in a monkey costume Juanita has made.

We arrive at the school at the appointed time where we are greeted by at least 50 assorted elephants, lions, African villagers and, of course, numerous other monkeys. As parents of a young pupil we

Spring in the Air

get to walk with our daughter in the parade on its route through the streets of Castres.

It's a movie-set moment. The police are the directors, closing down streets and escorting the parade as we move through the set, the narrow, cobblestone *rues* bordered by shops and houses. As we walk we make a huge racket thanks to our collection of shakers, not to mention whistles and general cheering. Confetti fills the air and the locals, like movie fans, lean out of windows or stand in their doorways and cheer as we, the stars of the show, pass by.

It's a great occasion for the children, and Eva loves every moment of her monkey business. The whole experience feels so wonderfully and typically French. Hell, they do this sort of thing all the time, don't they! Almost any occasion is an excuse to have a party. The combination of sun, heat and cheering children puts everyone in a fiesta mood, which makes the experience even more exceptional. I guess too that Castres is small enough for such occasions to be just the right amount of fun. Unlike big-city celebrations, anything that happens here, and where a crowd is involved, is never overbearing. It's not too small a town either because there seem to be the right amount of people to ensure proceedings are lively. Bring on summer I say. There's a definite spring in my step these days — despite the occasional twinge from my hamstring.

La cuisine Kiwi. Kiwi kai. The warm weather encourages us to entertain more. Juanita and I have always enjoyed having friends over for dinner and we pool our talents to come up with various Kiwi culinary delights we're sure will impress our guests. We dish up bacon and egg pie, pavlova (of course), New Zealand lamb (also of course), which we are able to buy at the local supermarket and which we serve with homemade mint jelly, and various kinds of kumara salads. Thankfully, all our efforts find appreciative stomachs.

We've also found an Asian supermarket so I'm able to stock up on all the ingredients for one of my favourite Japanese dishes — sushi. It's a big hit with our friends.

Meat is something of an issue. Our French, Argentinean and Spanish friends are huge meat eaters. In fact, not to serve a meat dish would be considered outrageous. So despite pies, salads and sushi, we always let our guests know there will be meat served during the course of a meal. It's hard to go past cooking a roast, and especially when our Latin friends get such obvious enjoyment from it.

Among our household goods that were shipped from New Zealand to France, we included a few bottles of New Zealand wine and they're being met with approval from our discerning French friends. As I write this, I'm wondering how on earth I'm going to be able to fill all the orders I'm being given. Any time I mention I'm returning to New Zealand for a few weeks between seasons, I get asked if I'll bring some wine back to France. It's not looking good for my baggage allowance. Excess here we come! I can't see the club forking out for bags containing wine rather than rugby gear. Or then again . . . maybe if I offer them some of the contents? Hmm . . .

Nous sommes en train de refaire les peintures. *We are doing some decorating.* At last! The time has come to drag our home into the 21st century. Because we're going to be living here for another year or two we desperately want to lose our 1980s décor and make our own mark on the house. We'd prefer something a little less in your face than what's there now and fortunately our landlord agrees to come to the party. He will have some of the rooms redecorated.

As part of the agreement, he is happy to organise the decorators if we will do the preparation work and repaint the hall and foyer walls. It's the one area of the house we can't agree on and, strangely enough (we certainly don't understand it), he seems quite attached to the wallpaper there with its huge floral pattern in shades of garish green, pink and beige. But although we can persuade him to let us cover the wallpaper, he isn't prepared to let us go to work on the feature wall that is, in our opinion *and* being polite, of the most questionable decorating taste. The wall is covered in a material. Pink material. At this stage, negotiations continue and our good friend Laurence is going to bat for us.

The workmen chosen by the landlord appear to be efficient. Well, that's our initial impression. We were a bit worried they might be typically French and so only turn up on an annoyingly irregular basis. But they put in huge work days, don't stop for morning or afternoon tea, and seem happy to call a halt once a day when they take a couple of hours' siesta around noon.

They're not great conversationalists, either among themselves or with us. One day Juanita is in the kitchen preparing a meal when the painter comes in, and without so much as a word in her direction starts laying sheets over everything, sets up his ladder and starts to prep and paint the ceiling. Dinner is quickly abandoned because of the debris and we end up having takeaways as our *plat du jour*. Do the painters look the least bit concerned? No, they never even bat an eyelid despite the fact they've just ruined our meal. I find it quite bizarre given that food is widely regarded by the French as their most important national treasure and the preparation of it taken extremely seriously.

Le Rugbyman

Despite the fact we don't smoke, that there are small children in the house and there's nothing to suggest our home is a smoke-friendly environment (not an ashtray in sight), the painters don't hesitate to light up. The first time it happens Juanita thinks the house is on fire and rushes from room to room trying to find the source of the fire. She finds one of the painters puffing away while he's using turps. We appreciate the work they're doing but we'll be relieved to see them collect up their ladders and paints and carry them out our door the last time.

As it turns out, it may take a while to make our final goodbyes. Good workmen — yes. Consistent — no. They finish the wallpapering and painting of the ceiling but then disappear before they've completed work on one of the bedroom floors. Thankfully, it's a guestroom and we're not in a great hurry to move furniture in there, but it's an inconvenience all the same. We were told the job would take only two days but time is ticking on. Am I surprised? I guess not. In the end they're living up exactly to my expectations.

Eventually, the floor man comes to finish the job. It takes him only one day and he does a good job, although he's not without his idiosyncrasies. Juanita's in the kitchen and she notices dogs in our yard. She rushes outside, tells them to *allez, allez,* and then realises they might actually belong to our workman. They do, and in a gesture of goodwill she fills a container with water for them and leaves them to enjoy the yard.

We go out for lunch and return to find the dogs making themselves very much at home. In fact, it's as though they've moved in. But although we love dogs we can't keep pets, especially indoors. Eva is severely allergic and she has an almost anaphylactic reaction to dogs.

Spring in the Air

As we shoo the animals out of the house we can only shake our heads in wonder at how giving the dogs a bowl of water translated into the bloke thinking we'd be happy to have them wandering around indoors.

His mindset tallies with so much that I've experienced on the rugby front. The way the French can leapfrog to conclusions, and quite different ones to what I'm often expecting, is just another part of the great learning curve that moving to a foreign country is all about.

13
Getting Away from it All

Sur la route encore. On the road again. It is with a lighter heart that I head to the Valencia region during the first week of March. Spring is literally in the air, which means the weather is warmer, the days are lengthening, and I am looking forward to getting out of Castres for a couple of weeks, especially given that I am still plagued with hamstring problems. If it wasn't for the injury cloud hanging over me I'd be able to say with real confidence that life as a rugby player has never seemed so good. And despite the injury it's not that bad. Here we are about to set off for Spain, this time venturing south of Barcelona. Juanita's mother, Elaine, is coming with us and this enforced break is going to be a wonderful opportunity for all of us to explore a little bit more of Europe.

Valencia is one of the biggest and liveliest cities in Spain and now also the base for America's Cup holders Team Alinghi of Switzerland.

Hopefully, we'll be able to return here in 2007 and watch Team New Zealand race in what will be the 32nd challenge for the America's Cup. It would be great to watch the Kiwis take the cup back home from there.

Valencia is on the Mediterranean coast and 350 km south of Barcelona. Because of the distance we decide to break the journey and spend the first night in Barcelona. Food is uppermost in my mind when we arrive, especially as it's at a time most self-respecting Kiwis would call their dinner hour. But of course we're not in New Zealand and we know there's at least another hour to wait until restaurants open their kitchens. I try to ignore my protesting stomach as we go for a quiet walk around the streets to stretch the legs. The girls are certainly in need of some fresh air and exercise. Thankfully, Spain, like France, is very child friendly. It intrigues me that in both these countries you find children's playgrounds dotted throughout the towns and cities, and as we watch Inez and Eva play, getting rid of their pent-up energies after being cooped up in the car, I'm grateful for these purpose-built distractions from grumbling tummies.

After dinner we settle in for the evening, excited about tomorrow and the fact we'll be seeing yet another new place. It's amazing how much sightseeing we've managed to fit in to the few months we've been in France. If the rugby isn't always coming up to my expectations, the opportunities to take off and explore most definitely are. It's what I'd dared to hope we could do and, touch wood, so far, so good.

The Spanish countryside is very different to the lush green pastures and prettiness of France. About 60 per cent of Spain is high country and on the journey south from Barcelona to Valencia we pass through countryside that is quite rocky, ochre-red and arid.

Getting Away from it All

I've read that the Spanish terrain is diverse and that lush valleys and meadows can be found far from here in the south and also towards the west. Temperatures in early March are warmer than we've been used to in Castres and it helps to put us in holiday mood.

The warmth appears to have ignited a festive spark among the locals too, and we drive past towns and villages strewn with fairy lights and colourful decorations hanging on walls and in the streets. Fireworks displays light the sky and it's as though all the country has put on its party clothes to give the Meeuws family the warmest of Spanish welcomes.

In fact, it really is festival time in the Valencia region. Our trip happens to coincide with the annual fire festival, *Las Fallas*. Huge and brightly coloured papier-mâché monuments called *ninots* or *Fallas* figurines have pride of place at the festivals. Apparently the making of them employs quite a number of people all year round and their creations, amazingly ornate figures, are designed to mock current customs, fashion and traditions. The city of Valencia is home to some 750,000 people (all of whom seem to be out on the town tonight) and the streets are literally throbbing with noise and colour. The sound of marching bands, parades and fireworks fill the air and the streets are packed with people dressed in traditional Spanish costume, all intent on enjoying themselves. It's an amazing experience to be part of. On the final night of festivities, 19 March, also Father's Day and known as St Joseph's Day in Spain, all but one of the *ninots* will be burned in an enormous bonfire-like blaze. This ritual marks the end of the winter months and the start of spring. The most popular *ninot* (don't ask me how they arrive at a consensus) is saved and will spend the rest of its days as an exhibit in the Museum of the Ninot along with the figurines saved from fires of past years.

Le Rugbyman

The entire region is in party mode. Further down the coast of Valencia and the Costa Blanca there are more celebrations going on that coincide with our visit. The history of the Moors and Christians provides another excuse for more revelry, and this time mock negotiations and battles are enacted before the grand finale of yet another parade. It's a sensory feast with more huge figurines decorating and adorning the streets, more fireworks, music and parades. The place is alive with colour. It's dazzling, almost overwhelming, and completely and wonderfully foreign. We are delighted to be in the right place at the right time and, as an experience, what can I say except that it is magic.

We don't intend to spend all our time in Valencia. Our destination is Gandia, another hour's drive south of the city of Valenica and located on the shores of the Mediterranean. There are two parts to the town, Gandia city *olde* and *Playa* about five minutes from the beach. It's this area closer to the coast that caters for the tourist influx throughout the European summers. Known as the Brits' home away from home, the high-rise apartments and shiny new hotels with their casinos dominate the skyline. It's all a far cry from the quaint farms and houses with dull terracotta roofing that I've become so used to.

However, there are advantages of being in an area frequented by the British: firstly, they sell baked beans and mint sauce in the supermarkets and, secondly, most of the Spaniards here, aside from speaking their local Spanish dialect, can also speak English. This is of huge comfort to me. Having to come to grips with the Spanish language on top of my pidgin French would be, I fear, a language overload!

Like France, Spain too has its localised provincial languages. In

Getting Away from it All

Castres, which is in the province of Tarn, the local language and identity is Occitan and there is a total immersion school where students are taught in the language and about its culture.

There is a division of opinion about the local language. Some say it isn't a dialect or a *patois* but a true language in its own right. There are even claims that Occitan was the European language of the Middle Ages. To an educated ear, Occitan is closer to the languages of Catalan, Spanish, Italian and Portuguese than French. Just my luck to live in an area of France where the local lingo has more in common with the neighbouring countries!

Of course, Tarn is not the only province in France to have its own dialect (or true language depending on your point of view). These dialects are an important source of identity for the peoples of various regions and they work hard to ensure they will be preserved. I've already had some experience of the emotion exuded by these dialects, or languages. Only a few weeks ago I was over on France's west coast among the Basque people. I've visited an area known as the Roussillon or Catalan country, which borders the Basque region and takes in the Pyrénées, including Andorra, Perpignon and down through the Catalonian province in Spain. Beyond the borders of Catalunya is Valencia and there, like France, the local language and culture of each of the Spanish provinces provide their strong source of identity. Everywhere I travel provides glimpses of other cultures, and whether I'm meeting with locals or simply observing them, hearing people talk brings home just how much one's language is an integral part of what we are — as a citizen of a country, from a region or as an individual. Maybe that old chestnut, it's not what you say but how you say it, has more substance to it than I'd ever imagined.

Le Rugbyman

Habiter le rêve. Living the dream. Having not played rugby for some time because of my hamstring injury, it's important I keep training and increasing my workload on my leg. The white sand beach and its boulevard make a perfect running track each morning or night. As I quite literally pound the pavement or run along the beach I almost need to pinch myself to make sure I'm not dreaming.

'Hey look at me!' I manage to stop myself from shouting, 'Here's Kees Meeuws, bona fide Auckland Westie running along the shores of the Mediterranean!' Who would have thought it?

Our bonus while on holiday is having a built-in babysitter. Elaine wants to spend time with her mokopuna (grandchildren) and Juanita and I like to explore the countryside and have some time to ourselves — something that has proved impossible since moving to France. Elaine, bless her, comes to the party in exactly the right way. We're given our marching orders — to go and enjoy ourselves, to relax. We don't need asking twice!

First on our agenda is a day trip to the city of Valencia. Wow! It is a beautiful city with plenty to see and do and we soon decide that our one-day trip will have to become at least two. In the city centre there is an enormous aquarium. We'll have to bring the girls here because we know they'll love looking at the dolphins, beluga whales and sharks, just to name a few of the attractions here.

We take time out in the middle of the day and have our siesta in the Plaza la Reina. It's a good opportunity to stop for lunch and sample traditional Spanish tapas and wash them down with some of the very passable local wine. Being tourists, we decide to pick a few sites to visit from the many available. Funnily enough, all the ones we choose are in close proximity to the shopping area. Have wife, will shop comes to mind.

However, neither of us can go past the *Catedral Metropolitana*, or Metropolitan Cathedral, with its amazing mix of buildings from eras we can only dream of. It's like walking through the pages of history books as we explore these monuments to the Romanesque, Gothic, Renaissance and Baroque periods. The *El Miguelete* belltower dates back to the 14th century. In the Holy Grail chapel the bones of various saints are on display, some still sporting their jewellery. It makes for slightly gruesome viewing, standing there gazing at a severed arm with rings still on the bony fingers. Juanita and I are not sure what we think of this display of sainted skulls, bones and even leathery skin. We leave the gloom of the cathedral behind and set off towards the Plaza Ayuntamiento. A sudden cacophony of thunderous explosions, sounding like mini bombs going off, startles us out of tourism mode. But there are no bombs, only fireworks. The noise is deafening. As we walk on we can only shake our heads and wonder why anyone would organise a display of what seems like about $50,000 worth of fireworks for the middle of a warm and sunny day. Who will see them? But then we find out that this display is not the main event, but merely a rehearsal for this evening.

It takes 10 minutes for the noise to die down and we arrive at the plaza just as the last few rockets take to the skies. As the thick smoke slowly lifts we see hundreds of people watching and cheering, along with a curiously large number of medical staff. We guess they're on standby in case of fireworks mishaps.

Some of the men and women in the crowd are dressed in traditional costume. It's a wonderful sight and another one of those picture postcard moments where I catch myself smiling, basking in the sunshine and the knowledge that real-life Spain is just as I'd imagined it to be. I feel so fortunate to be a part of yet another Spanish fiesta, or, as we say in France, *la fête*.

Le Rugbyman

The following day we head south to the Costa Blanca. Alicante, known as the City of Light, is on today's list of places to explore. It's the second largest city in Valencia with a population of around 300,000, and its situation on the coast means it is both a tourist Mecca and a port.

It has a rich history dating back three thousand years and as in Valencia there are many monuments to visit. As we park the car at Postiguet beach, we look upwards to the summit of the 166-m Mount Benacantil where the Castillo de Santa Bárbara, or Santa Bárbara Castle, stands. I spy stairs and a road winding their way up to the top of the not inconsiderable hill, but as I'm about to mention to Juanita that we have an hour's hike to look forward to she happens to point out a conveniently placed lift hollowed out of the hillside. Suddenly our trek to the castle is looking like a walk, or should I say, ride, in the park.

From sea level this monument doesn't look like all that much. Just some old ruins I assume. But as soon as I step out of the elevator I quickly change my tune. It's the real Spanish casa — courtyards, palm trees and cobblestone paths. It's another wow! The castle, most of it built during the 16th century, occupies a strategic position in Alicante, and its view takes in the entire city and the whole Alicante plain. No wonder it was so popular with the Iberians, Romans and the Spanish. It's even been under attack from the French Armada.

But today it's a peaceful and awe-inspiring place. Apart from the architecture, I'm delighted to find that the castle houses the Alicante Sculpture Symposium that is devoted to international sculpture and contemporary art. The setting could not be more perfect. As I take in the breathtaking vista I also get to indulge in one of my passions — art, and sculpture at that. Can it get any better?

Getting Away from it All

Eventually we take a break from the sightseeing and settle down for a mini siesta at the castle grounds café. It's a perfect Mediterranean spring day, about 26 degrees, and I can understand why Spain's coastal cities and villages are swamped with holiday-makers from other, more northern European countries and the British Isles and Ireland during summer months.

But my rumbling stomach interrupts my reverie. It's the sort of reality check I enjoy. If my system's telling me it's hungry I'd better indulge in that Mediterranean gastronomical delight — seafood. Well, it would be rude not to.

After a leisurely and delicious lunch, we walk along the Paseo de la Explanada. It's a beautiful waterfront promenade that in 1957 was paved with more than six and a half million small red, cream and black marble tiles. It must have taken a whole lot of man-hours to complete the job but, from a Kiwi tourist's point of view, it was well worth the effort. We stroll to our car and then head back up the coast.

As we wind down the steep roads into Calpe we're confronted by a massive rock. It's impossible to miss. The Penon de Ifac, or the Rock of Ifach, peaks at 332 m. The rock is a nature reserve but a walking track has been made for those willing to embark on the hour-long trek to the top. Juanita and I are keen to conquer this obelisk but the locals put us off. They warn us that our footwear isn't suitable and that to make it all the way to the summit tramping shoes are essential. So we settle for the next best thing, which is to find a café by the sea, eat ice-cream and watch those who have come, better prepared than us, climb the rock. Yep, definitely a more sensible idea!

The next few days are spent exploring Gandia. While there, we discover that Gandia is the Spanish capital of shoes. Of course, no mention of this was made when the holiday was originally booked and despite my wife's protests to the contrary, I am sure I've been duped! Umpteen pairs of shoes later, mostly gifts for family back home (yeah, right), I hear Juanita muttering something about 'when in Rome…' I'm not sure exactly how that relates to shoe shopping but after this experience there's no way I'm letting her loose in places like Milan or Rome. I think we should stick to culture. It's way less expensive.

The most cultural thing we manage to do in Gandia is visit their famous Ducal Palace, also known as Palace of the Borja. Famous for being a residence for both royalty and the Catholic hierarchy, it too has a long and tumultuous history. Looking at it, it's almost impossible to believe that at one time the palace had become little more than a ruin. The Jesuits bought it at public auction in 1887 and then, almost two centuries later, the palace was declared an historic and artistic monument. During the 1990s a major restoration project was carried out. Like so many of the monuments throughout Europe, this palace is now, thankfully, another example of incredible architecture and furnishings. And as with every place we've been fortunate enough to visit, it is maintained by locals with an immense pride in their heritage.

We spent our last day in the province in Valencia at the *L'Oceanogràfic* or, in English, the Oceanographic. The largest marine park in Europe, it's also high up the wow factor list. Made up of nine thematic buildings, each represents a different marine system. From the wetlands and mangrove swamps to the Arctic Circle with its beluga whales and walruses, this place has it all. The architecture reminds me of a space-age film set with spheres and arches emerging out of outdoor pools and gardens.

Eva and Inez are entranced. It's a thoroughly enjoyable experience for young children and adults alike. For me, the highlight is seeing the large ocean mammals, but for the girls it's hard to go past the dolphins. One dolphin keeps watching and following Inez. When she moves, it moves with her and every so often it squirts water at us. I'm amazed that even from within the tank it can still see her and it seems to be intrigued and maybe even protective towards my younger daughter.

Part of me is pained at seeing these highly intelligent creatures kept in captivity. But I'm also guilty of feeling a little hedonistic. It's a real buzz to be able to take in the whole oceanographic experience — and that includes being able to see up close wonderful creatures such as the dolphins.

We take lots of photos and then a couple of Italian guys approach and ask for my autograph and if I'd have my photo taken with them. The same thing happened when we were in Barcelona.

That rugby is so global never ceases to amaze me. When I think of rugby, New Zealand is the first place that springs to mind, but since I've moved overseas I've been approached in Andorra, Spain and obviously France with people coming up and wanting to shake my hand or to get my autograph and pose for photos with them. I find it humbling and also flattering. In fact I'm blown away that, out of context, they recognise my face and obviously enjoy the sport so much. Rugby has certainly opened many doors in my life and I hope it continues to do so.

14
Trials and Tribulations

Avancez. Go forward. It's taken more than a month, but by the end of March I'm declared fit to play against Narbonne. The match will be played away from home — always extra cause for concern — but right now I'm more intent on making sure the body is up to the rigours of rugby than worrying about the mind games that preoccupy most of my team-mates and training staff prior to each outing.

I promise myself I will be cautious at trainings and not push the body too hard, too early. The last thing I want to do is suffer a recurrence of my bothersome hamstring injury. I decide I'll ease myself through the trainings until the last one of the week when I plan to give it 100 per cent. However, my plans come unstuck right at the start. As soon as I touch the ball I find myself throwing caution to the wind, the ball is in my hands, I spy a space in front of me and I can't help myself . . . I go for it. Nothing happens!

What a marvellous feeling! From that moment on I train normally and with confidence.

Training goes well all week — a good sign, because there's a lot riding on this next match. A win will put us up into the top four and also in the running for a place in the French championship playoffs as well as securing us, mathematically, within the top six and thus guaranteeing us a place in next season's Heineken Cup competition. We spend time analysing the Narbonne team, its strengths and its weaknesses, and we train to a game plan we believe can bring us this much-needed victory.

C'est la victoire de l'esprit sur la matière. It's a case of mind over matter. But it's in our analyses that we seem to get things so badly wrong. Despite being a part of this team for more than half a season, I'm still amazed by our capacity to analyse who we'll beat, who we can beat, and who we've already beaten before we run onto the pitch. This habit of effectively counting our chickens before they hatch seems to result in only one team ending up with egg on their faces — ours!

I have a strong suspicion that the culture of over-analysing runs throughout French rugby, and that the only difference between one club and the next is how all this theorising is managed.

With Castres, our coaches regard all home games as win certainties, and the opposition as a mere and not terribly worrisome distraction. Before each captain's run they sit around and discuss the game as if we've already won it and then, moving quickly on — given that this one's in the bag — 'let's start analysing next week's game'. And then, after they're done with our game(s), they make a point of analysing every other team in the competition and how they're likely to play, who will win, who will lose and how all these permutations are going to affect overall placings on the competition ladder.

What's with all this hypothesising? Why not keep things real simple and think only about what's immediately in front of us — the next game — and take it from there. Let's be all about beating Narbonne!

Ferme-la! Shut up! Immediately prior to running out on the pitch at the Parc des Sports et de l'Amitié our coaches insist on giving us a speech that seems to go along the familiar and badly scripted lines of already having won the match. Although we're playing away from home, remember *nos amis* that Narbonne lie five places beneath us on the table and a win is therefore *inévitable*. I desperately want to speak up and let these guys know how ridiculous it is to take something like winning a yet-to-be-played rugby match for granted.

The only thing I'm positive about is that this sort of talk is a negative. Once our boys are told the game is in the bag they switch off. I've seen it happen already this season and I get that sinking feeling that today is going to turn out to be a bad day at the office. Don't get me wrong, I'm all for positive imagery, but I think the approach being taken by our coaches is wrong. It's breeding complacency within the side instead of instilling a match-winning boost of confidence.

And what do you know? We play like dogs. As has happened in previous away matches, the team pays little heed to the game plan we worked so hard to get right earlier in the week. Of course, there are a few of us out on the pitch trying to play as we trained, but it's to no avail. Tonight, too many of the team don't turn up, mentally. All our points come from the boot of fullback Romain Teulet but by halftime we're 10 points behind.

Then five minutes into the second half I suddenly find myself cooling my heels on the sideline. I'm sinbinned for taking out my opposition prop. I've been on top of him all game and he's obviously had enough so he gives me a nudge. But he's picked on the wrong man at the wrong moment. I'm full of pent-up frustration due to the dispiriting lack of enthusiasm being shown by my team-mates and I retaliate. Too late I realise what I've done. I'm not proud of myself but there's no taking it back.

There is one consolation. From the bench I notice our boys fire up and finally they turn up to play ball. But we're too far behind and when the final whistle goes we've notched up another away loss, 12–25.

De quoi parliez-vous? What were you talking about? After the game there's the usual press conference and I hear my name along with another couple of players being spat out by our coach Christian Gajan. I don't know what's being said but I get the impression he's not showering us with compliments.

Bad news is just the fodder the local papers love and they have a field day. I find out soon enough what's been said when a friend translates the articles for me. I'm livid. According to the reports, the coach blames me for the loss because I gave away a crucial penalty.

I find the news hard to stomach on a couple of levels. When the penalty was awarded we were seven points down and yes, that made it 10, but it's not like we'd closed to within a point or two of Narbonne or were looking in danger of scoring tries. In fact, it turned out to be another game in which we failed to cross the opposition line. Secondly, all season the coach had been saying that any criticisms stay in-house and if there are problems they'll be sorted out by the team and with the best interests of the team foremost.

Trials and Tribulations

I have a full head of steam up by the time I confront Christian and I have a go at him about what I perceive as his hypocrisy. He lets me shoot my mouth off and then tells me his comments after the game were misconstrued and that what he actually said is the less experienced members of the team are adversely affecting those of us with more experience, that they're lowering the standard of play. In his opinion we're being forced to play down to their standards rather than them raising theirs. I accept his comments in good faith and we're friends again.

En état de choc. At state of shock. But just as I'm coming back down to earth, tremors of earthquake proportions shake the team's foundations. The coach and trainer are fired and then Christian is reinstated the following day.

But our trainer Robert Froissard does not get a recall. There's a bit of history between him and our forwards' coach Christophe Urios. That these two haven't been seeing eye to eye has been obvious to everyone for some time, and with the current tension in the squad it was only a matter of time before it boiled over.

Prior to the game against Narbonne, when I'd just come back from injury and so too had fellow prop Justin Fitzpatrick, Mauricio Reggiardo was told there was no place for him in the starting lineup, despite his having a good match against Bourgoin. Mauricio didn't take the news well. In fact, he refused to take part in the training that had been assigned to him and went off and did his own thing. Christophe then began quizzing Mauricio about his lack of training with the rest of us but before he could answer, Robert butted in and told Christophe to go away and not to talk to Mauricio until he'd completed his drill.

Christophe told Robert to keep his 'big' nose out of it or get punched and Robert responded with a cheeky comment about punching Christophe's 'big' jaw. The next thing I know, Christophe has indeed cracked Robert on the nose, flattening him.

Meanwhile, we're all running up and down doing our warm-up drill, heads straight but watching out the corner of our eyes, not wanting to be caught staring but not wanting to miss this scuffle between two of our trainers.

Then, in what I consider to be in typical French style, Christophe walks away from Robert and comes over to us, and we continue the session without so much as a word being uttered as to what has taken place.

So, we lose our trainer. But although Christian's reinstatement is seen as positive news, there are more shocks in store. Before training, the club's CEO Pierre Yves Revol and some of his sidekicks take the opportunity to inform several of the players that their contracts will not be renewed for next season.

I am shocked and disgusted. I know the French are an emotional race, but this kind of behaviour is ridiculous. One team-mate is told he will have to wait another three weeks, until after our game against Stade Français in Paris, to find whether he gets a new two-year contract or is made redundant. Do the powers-that-be seriously imagine that having an axe hanging over his head is going to act as an incentive to make him play better? Is this roller-coaster of emotion over reason to be my lot too during my time in France? It makes the future seem like a minefield: trip up or take a wrong step and your whole career may just blow up in your face.

Perhaps things will be better next season. The rumour-mill is in overdrive and all the talk is that our new coach for next season, Laurent

Seigne, runs a tight ship and is not a man who takes kindly to being pushed around by club management. If only administrators would do just that — administrate. It's always been my opinion that these people whose primary concern should be the running of the club do not try to flex their muscles by attempting to control how games are played or involve themselves in the hiring and firing of coaches and players. A coach should be allowed to decide on his team and his game plan.

Maybe it sounds as though I'm living *un cauchemar*, a nightmare; I must confess I love all the intrigue. In the back of my mind I hold tight to the words of reassurance from those who've gone before me and survived their first-season experiences. They've all said that while the first season is crap, the second is superb. I hope so and if it holds true, then there will be much to look forward to with Castres in 2005–2006.

Despite this season's ups and downs I am more convinced than ever that, were the French ever to adopt the same sort of professional mindset and organisation that makes the Super 12 such a success, it would be a case of look out world rugby! I'm in no doubt that the French have the ability to dominate rugby on a global scale thanks to their wonderful natural talents, skills and enthusiasm.

But their lack of professionalism is hampering their advancement. I can only speculate as to why they seem to pick and choose the games they perform in. Maybe it's an inherently French attitude, and maybe it will be an impossible trait to change. But if they ever get serious . . . watch out!

Nous sommes logés à la même enseigne. We're in this together. The loss to Narbonne and the flurry of hirings and firings results in an impromptu training camp. We're heading to Soreze, a beautiful village not far from Castres. But we won't be doing any sightseeing. I'm anticipating a thrashing out of our problems and probably a whole lot more navel gazing as to where we're going wrong. If you ask me, it's all a little late in the season, a storm in a teacup sort of thing, the result of losing a game we'd been told prior to kick-off was already won.

I do think team bonding is a good thing, but it's something that needs to be worked on throughout a season and not thrust at us as a last-resort type of scenario in the hope we'll suddenly start winning.

And neither are our problems just about the team and the way we gel. There's a much bigger picture to look at — why we fail to stick to a game plan and how successfully completing basic tasks would go a long way to making us more competitive.

As I pack my bags and prepare to head away there's little to suggest this training camp is going to be a success. The boys are disillusioned about having to spend another couple of days away from home and I worry about whether it's going to pull us apart rather than bring us together.

Happily, my fears prove groundless. In our first training we concentrate on defence, and in particular where it went wrong during the game against Narbonne. We train as a team too, which is a departure from the norm. Usually we split up, the forwards doing our thing, the backs doing theirs. It's encouraging that we're finally working as a unit. But not all the time: the coach then organises backs against forwards, one defending and one attacking, and the competitive edge in all of us comes out to play. We're having fun too! This is so much more like trainings in New Zealand where the rivalry between backs and forwards is encouraged. It's such a normal and natural process in rugby and one that's conducive to a team's performance, everyone trying to get one up on the other bloke and thus creating a healthy competitiveness within the team.

Mind you, from where I'm standing, it seems that the forwards are doing a lot of extra work such as lineouts and scrums while the backs are simply standing around in a huddle and discussing what they are planning to do. In my next life, I plan to return as a back!

Our afternoon becomes an extension of the morning's session. The gruelling, back-breaking training we're expecting never eventuates and suddenly there's a sprightliness about the team that's been absent for some time.

Prior to dinner we have a team meeting and the coach proposes a *challenge fou*, a crazy challenge, which is where he declares our target for the rest of the season should be to win five out of the six games left. He reckons it's possible as long as 'everyone swims in the same direction'.

In order to achieve our goal, he says we must eliminate the sub-groups that have sprung up within the squad. Then he takes a seat and the floor is open to anyone who wants to have a say. A few of the boys take advantage of the invitation and home truths are verbalised. Everyone is in agreement with what is said.

That night over dinner the cliques finally disappear. We have Frenchmen sitting alongside Poms, Argentineans with the French, all of us chatting and swapping banter as guys do. The changes are all positive and I'll never know whether it's the result of our on-the-field trainings or the clearing of the air, but, finally, we seem to have a proper and healthy team environment.

Dans les moments cruciaux. When the chips are down. Anyway, we have our own method of team bonding and it has nothing to do with rugby. We organise games of poker that coincide with our wives or partners going out for dinner. It's a good excuse for us to catch up and get to know each other away from the training or playing pitch.

There's a school of eight to 10 blokes, and a couple of the boys bring along their professional poker chips, which all helps to add to the ambience. There's no standing on ceremony and everyone is expected to bring along his choice of snack food, wine or beer. It's not big money either and our entry fee is set at a flat 20 euros.

It's a lot of fun, men just being men. But the sessions often run on into the wee hours because we're a competitive bunch and, if the chips are down, well, it always seems like a sensible idea to try and recoup the losses! Either that or the wife arrives back and declares game over!

15

The Good, the Bad and the Ugly

Faire son chemin. To make good. Post-Narbonne we need a solid performance, and I require an especially good one given that there's a photographer here taking some shots for this book. I'd hate him to come all this way for nothing!

Fortunately, fate chooses to be kind today against Brive. Our scrum dominates, the backs play well and, to a degree, we follow through with the game plan. With the platform set and early points on the board thanks to a converted try, opportunities soon present themselves for me to demonstrate just what a try-scoring demon I can be. The game is only eight minutes old when I dot down for the first time and it's the result of an 'if at first you don't succeed, try and try again' type scenario. Twice, I'm stopped just short of the line but there's not going to be anything or anyone denying me my third charge at the line. We're into our fourth phase of play and seven metres out when I pick and go, dashing between two opposition players, the legs pumping as fast as I can make them, and I dive over the line. Our fullback Romain Teulet adds his second conversion of the game and we're 14 points up for none conceded.

Brad Fleming adds a try in the 37th minute and with Romain raising the flags for the conversion we go to halftime with a healthy 24–6 lead.

But matters go quickly pear-shaped for yours truly. Only minutes into the second spell I'm yellow-carded. I can't believe it — two sinbinnings in two weeks! It happens during an incident in a lineout. It's Brive's ball to the lineout and as the ball comes in I step into their lineout just as their lifter loses control of their jumper who then topples over my head. The ref takes exception and sends me off for dangerous play. I have to accept that it can't have looked good but there was no malice on my part. It was, I swear, a total accident.

Wracking up yellow card offences is not something I'd like to make a habit of either. Throughout my career I've never been red-carded and I think I notched up no more than two yellow cards in my 45 All Black appearances. One was against the French and another against South Africa in our 2003 Tri Nations encounter. It's never a good feeling to be forced off the pitch, although on that particular day I can't say my team-mates missed me all that much. We won 52–16.

Back to today, however, and the Brive kicker successfully converts the penalty that results from my infringement, but one minute later their loosehead prop Pierre Capdevielle negates their one-man player advantage by copping a yellow card.

By the time my 10 minutes in the sin bin are over the teams have exchanged one more penalty goal each and we're still comfortably ahead 27–12. We surge ahead as the result of a try to David Barrier and then I decide to make amends for my perceived misdemeanour by scoring a second try. This time we're hot on attack and make our way 30 to 40 metres upfield through good use of the ball. A ruck forms about 10 metres from the line and 20 metres in from the right-hand side of the pitch. I've made the decision to do a pick and go before I look up and when I do, whoops, there are more opposition players in front of me than I expect. But the ball is in my hands at this stage and I'm not about to back down. I decide the best way forward is straight ahead and charge towards the line. With three guys on my back I scrape over to notch up a try. Romain adds the conversion and we have 37 points on the board. With 10 minutes remaining we lose our shape and let Brive in for two converted tries, but at the final whistle we're still ahead, 37–29.

We leave the field in an upbeat mood. Sure, next week we have to play away against crack team Stade Français, but today's game has been a good morale booster for us.

Le mauvais ... The bad ... The last thing I need in the run-up to the game against Stade Français is another injury scare but that's exactly what I get. And it's all thanks to a training accident. We're doing an attacking drill when one of my team-mates sticks out a knee and I take a tumble. The pain is incredible and at first I think I've done my ankle but tests reveal a haematoma on the shin. I'm told to rest.

At last, though, I receive the best medical treatment I've had since arriving here and have physio twice a day three days in a row. My usual physio is unavailable so an appointment is made for me to see someone else. I find my way to his rooms but as soon as I walk through the door I do a double-take. It's another time-warp moment.

Le Rugbyman

As I look at the equipment I'm thinking 1960s (is Dr Kildare going to walk through the door any minute?) or maybe I've made it as far forward as the '70s. The physio's little chamber of horrors consists of assorted contraptions housed in steel mesh cubicles such as weighted sandbags with pulleys, old leather medicine balls and, wait for it, the *pièce de résistance* is the very first-ever leg extension machine ever made! The tables are showing signs of serious wear, and rips and tears are covered over with duct tape. There's a strong smell of chlorine in the air. But, fortunately, the treatment I receive is very 21st century and I'm back running within two days.

As a team, we're travelling to Paris with high hopes of doing well against the European Cup finalists. It may be an order too tall to beat this side but all the indications are good. We have what is our best captain's run of the season, no dropped balls and with everything carried out at a high intensity. It's a short, sharp session but everyone does what is expected of them and they all turn up in the right place at the right time.

It's a big game in all senses. Pride is a major factor here. Parisians see themselves as the 'real' French, and in some ways I'm loath to disagree with them. So much of France is localised — history, languages, attitudes, foods and celebrations. It's easy to see why, from a foreigner's point of view (and a sentiment obviously shared by native Parisians), France is all about Paris with its iconic monuments, culture and renowned sense of style. On a more basic level, this game is about big city versus small town and, as with anywhere in the world, we're going to do anything we can to make the city boys sit up and take notice of us.

We leave Castres with a lot of baggage and I'm not talking bags here, I'm talking people, specifically administrative staff and board

The Good, the Bad and the Ugly

members — the fish-heads — who always put in an appearance when there's a big trip to be made.

The fish-head phenomenon is worldwide. Today it's off to Paris and, yes, it's great to have the support, just like it has been over previous years when, as an All Black, I've been heading away to Bledisloe Cup tests and World Cups. But isn't it strange that it's always on the really big occasions that, suddenly, the travelling party doubles in size!

But flight completed and out on the pitch, we're quickly brought down to earth. Despite our positive build-up to the match we end up playing too easily into Parisian hands, and this despite a positive start that sees us ahead by three points in as many minutes. Disappointingly, our discipline lets us down and the sophisticated city slickers are able to overcome our rather country-bumpkin performance. The first major blow is when our loose forward Paul Volley is sinbinned for a late tackle on halfback Agustin Pichot. I think it's a harsh decision, but, as I'm discovering over here, them's the breaks!

Throughout the season I've noticed that whenever someone is sent from the pitch — and all too often it's one of our forwards — there we are, one man short in the scrum, really up against it and about to be done over by the opposition. It doesn't matter where the opposing team is in relation to ours on the championship table — they could be the bottom side — but knowing we're a man down they will proceed to attack our weakened scrum as if they're the French champions. Every team here seems to have a really strong front row, and they're every bit and often tougher to play against than I'd been led to believe. It can sure make for a long, hard day at the office!

Le Rugbyman

The way of doing things in France is quite different to New Zealand when it comes to a team being a man down in scrum situations. Back home, if a forward is sent off and we have to set a scrum we usually load up the side we're trying to manipulate, to twist or turn the scrum to give us the advantage depending on where we are on the field. For example, if we're on the left side of the pitch we'll be aiming to twist the scrum right, and vice versa. In the middle of the field it will depend on what back moves are called, whether they're planning to go left or right.

But in France teams tend to load up their loosehead side no matter where they are on the field. It's taking some getting used to. Most other teams also wheel up their loosehead side, thus creating more pressure for me on the tighthead, and my energy expenditure goes through the roof. After every scrum I come out feeling like I've just competed in that rather bizarre Man v Horse v Mountain Bike marathon that is, just in case you don't know, the pride of Llanwrtyd Wells, which is, in case you don't know, officially the smallest town in Britain.

But back to Paris. We're actually leading 15–11 with 15 minutes to go in the second half when our other loose forward, Romain Froment, gets our second yellow card. There ends our chance of holding on to win the match. The Parisians close to within one point when the penalty is successfully converted and they go on to add a try, conversion and penalty for a 24–15 win that denies us even a bonus point.

I trudge off the pitch feeling extremely disappointed. My work rate has been huge, I know that, but I can't say I feel pleased with my performance, especially given the final result.

But others see my game quite differently. At the after-match both the CEO and head coach come up to me to congratulate me on the

The Good, the Bad and the Ugly

way I played. Even our forwards coach Christophe gives me three hearty pats on the back, his way of getting through the language barrier to let me know he thinks I've done well.

I'm baffled. Just a week ago I played on a winning side, made some storming runs and scored two tries, but today when I don't make any glamour moves or score any tries I seem to be more of a hit with the hierarchy!

I later hear that the match commentators reckoned only two of the Castres team could be considered to have turned up and played against Stade Français. One of them was yours truly.

Moche . . . Ugly . . . It's hotting up, quite literally, and the end of the season is nigh. Five games to go, summer is tantalisingly close and I'm starting to dream about al fresco dining, days spent at the local lakes and trips to the Med where, thanks to French friends, a holiday house in the small town of Gruisson has been made available to us.

But before I can start planning a dip in the warm waters of the Med I've got another trip back to Basque country and the Bay of Biscay to look forward to, although how we're going to perform against Biarritz is uncertain. Last weekend Biarritz lost their Heineken Cup semi-final match against our last adversaries, Stade Français, and you can guarantee that loss will only have served to fire them up for the match against Castres.

Well, that's *my* take on things. According to many of my French colleagues, Castres is more than likely to win this game because Biarritz will not be up for it mentally after suffering the disappointment of losing to Paris. It's like banging heads against the by-now much-dented brick wall! How often are we going to fall into the trap of winning the game before it's played?

Maybe I speak too soon because we dominate the early stages of the game and are three points up after Romain Teulet kicks a penalty goal midway through the half. But my propping partner Mauricio Reggiardo comes close to undoing all our good work when he is yellow-carded a couple of minutes later.

We're down to 13 players when our No 8 Jacques Deen is also sent to the sin bin, but fortunately Biarritz is unable to take advantage of their numbers superiority and although we're down two men at scrum time we seem unaffected. In fact we go further in front to lead 6–0.

But with 38 minutes gone Biarritz get on the scoring board with a try. It's not converted so we're in front at halftime. And I'd like to point out that this half lasted an extraordinary 57 minutes! I'm not optimistic about our chances because our play can only be considered as adequate and there's a long way still to go.

I don't get the impression that our coach is particularly positive either, given his halftime spiel. All I understand is the French *putang* every third or fourth word. It's been an easy one to learn given that it's the French equivalent of the f*** word. Christian orders our reserve prop and hooker to warm up because he plans to put them on 10 minutes into the second half.

Best laid plans and all that . . . any chance we have of winning the game evaporates with only two minutes of the second spell played. That's when Mauricio makes a head-high tackle and receives his second yellow card, which, of course, translates to an immediate red card and we're down to 14 men for the remainder of the game.

Mauricio, Mauricio, what were you thinking? Literally less than two hours before he's sent off, Mauricio was imparting impassioned words of wisdom and/or motivation to us. He's Argentinean and

The Good, the Bad and the Ugly

therefore highly emotional, and even more so at this time because his contract with Castres has not been renewed and these final games of the season are to be the last of his career.

Mauricio is something of a unique character. It doesn't matter whether he's dressed for training or in number ones, his attire is highly personalised — sleeves torn off shirts that are already frayed around the edges, and his unkempt long hair giving him the appearance of a crazy man. Add to that his on-field antics of the last couple of weeks . . . no, make that the whole season, have cost his team dearly. Yellow cards, he has plenty of those, and yes, red ones too; game suspensions — a given — and he gives away penalty after penalty.

I can recall playing against him in 2001, All Blacks versus the Pumas. He's a niggling bugger at the best of times and certainly not immune to using the choker hold and *not* letting go. During that 2001 match the All Black coaches dragged me from the field before I was yellow-carded (but not before I got a knee into Mauricio). We were at each other the entire time I was on the pitch, but only because I had no intention of backing down to him. He tried to gouge my eyes, was pulling at my jersey as he ran from scrums, trying to punch me at the bottom of rucks and generally doing all the annoying shit he's a master at.

I remember the game as being a particularly tight contest. We certainly couldn't afford to have anyone yellow-carded and it was only our No 8 Scott Robertson's late try that won us the game 24–20.

Fast-forward to 2005 and Mauricio's pre-match speech on how he wants to go out from rugby on a high. He's promising to play to the top of his game. Well, I think that's what he's saying. He's pretty near impossible to understand because as well as ranting in his shocking French (and according to his countrymen, his Spanish is

Le Rugbyman

just as unintelligible) he's bawling his eyes out. But even he can't live up to his own expectations, and despite all the talk and histrionics, he lets us down with his ill discipline.

For all of Mauricio's faults, though, it's impossible to dislike the man. He won't be lost from Castres either — the town that is. He owns one of the local watering holes and it has become a mini icon and popular meeting place.

With Mauricio gone, our heads drop and Biarritz play with renewed vigour. Once again, there's no way back for us from here as the home team runs in try after try, six being their final match tally. Although Brad Fleming dots down late in the game it's nothing more than a consolation effort for Castres and the final score is 40–13 to Biarritz.

I'm shattered after having to endure 50 minutes as part of a seven-man forward pack. Like last week, I feel I'm getting around the park well, hitting rucks, making covering tackles, doing my job, but doing it well. But for all that, I'm beginning to feel the toll of having played rugby almost non-stop since January 2004.

However, my efforts don't go unnoticed and for the third week running the *Midi Olympique* awards me a star. It's a rating system to indicate level of performance nationwide. There are one, two and three star categories and my aim is to give a three-star performance before I end my playing days in France. I appreciate the recognition and it certainly helps boost my motivation. I may be exhausted but the competitive spirit is most definitely not flagging.

As we head away from Biarritz I try not to be too downhearted about the game. But it's difficult. I look around me as our bus heads out of this beautiful resort town. The beaches look fantastic and so too the surf. Apparently, Biarritz was a favourite holiday spot for Napoleon the Third and his Spanish-born wife, the Empress Eugenie, and many buildings in the town were built in her honour.

As we head towards Castres I settle back and try to enjoy the journey. In a few weeks' time I'll be back here, but this time as a tourist. Juanita and I have a holiday planned. Just us, a few friends and as much sea and surf as we like. I can't wait.

16
Season's End

Enfin. Finally. And so the season is drawing to an end. I'm not quite sure if it's been a long or a short one — so much has happened. But when I think back to the selling of our house, packing up our belongings, having to decide what to leave behind and what to bring to France and then those whirlwind few days in November before I got on the plane, well, it seems like a lifetime ago.

If I thought life was moving fast then, the pace has hardly ever slowed since touching down on French soil. It's hard to believe all I've managed to pack in over the past six months — the people I've met and the places I've visited, both in France and further afield.

From a rugby point of view, this season has been a big learning curve. That Castres wants to succeed has never been called into question, although the way players, coaches and management have gone about trying to achieve their goals has not always been easy for me to understand, and that's without taking the language difficulties into consideration.

As I write this, I can look back on last weekend's game with a lot of satisfaction. We beat Montferrand 54–23, which in itself was cause for celebration. But on a more personal level, I think it was also my finest hour as a member of this team — and not just because I scored two tries during the game (I'm almost a back; well, maybe an honorary one) and won the player of the match award. I put a lot of thought into how to approach this match, and all week I'd been asking myself what it would take to get the French boys to perform at their best. The 1999 World Cup match, New Zealand against France, was playing on my mind. What made the French step up against us on that particular day?

A couple of the players in our team had played for France during that World Cup and had lined up against the All Blacks for that game so I took the opportunity to ask them about it. Their responses helped me to understand not only what it was that helped them to win but also gave me invaluable insight into how the French think, work and act.

Since I've been in France I've noticed a hierarchy, not only with my team-mates but out in civvie street as well. Within the team, some players — seniors — refuse to acknowledge others who would be considered of more junior status. If there's a reason for the top dogs' reluctance to slum it with the mongrels, it's one I've yet to fathom. And yet, in a way, it encapsulates the French people — the way they so openly show their disdain to anything or anyone they consider beneath them. There are the Parisians against the rest of France; there's the rude waiter or shop assistant who will treat the customer — especially a foreign one — like a disgusting bit of doggy-doo *until* a fuss is kicked up. But then, with the tables turned, he or she suddenly becomes the most obliging member of the service industry ever seen! It happens, it's part of French territory, but for those of us not used to these cultural nuances it provides constant challenges. How can you go along with the game when you don't even know it's being played? Sometimes it's a matter of working out who is trying to prove the other party wrong, who is trying to save face, and who is involved in some hierarchical struggle you weren't even aware existed.

According to my team-mates, back in 1999 the French regarded our haka as a threat and our performance of it equated to their having already lost face. Remember now, this is their mindset before the game has even commenced! In order to redeem themselves they played out of their skins and the winning of the match equated with turning the tables on us and, *voilà*, as a result they'd saved face.

I pondered this information and then I asked to be allowed to speak to the team before our game against Montferrand. I issued each team member with a challenge. I asked every man if he had the heart to play the 80 minutes of this match giving it 100 per cent. I also said we should forget about all the games we 'coulda, shoulda, woulda' won and to focus on the game at hand. Not the entire competition, forget about that — just *this* game. Did they have *le coeur*? Did they have the heart?

At halftime, when we were up by 19–6 (all our points to this stage coming from fullback Romain Teulet — a converted try and four penalties) I challenged the team once more. Did they have the guts and the heart to play out the second spell just as well as they had in the first half, if not better?

I told them the easy part was over and asked them if they still had the drive to finish this game the way they'd started, and that we needed to keep that momentum going until the final whistle sounded. Our reward for a solid 80-minute performance would be to walk off that pitch having achieved the result we wanted — and deserved. Enough said; the time had come to lead by example. Four minutes into that second spell I scored my first try of the day.

Looking back, that performance against Montferrand was, without doubt, our best of the season. By questioning the players' integrity I'd forced them to question themselves. The French especially felt they had a point to prove — to save face — and they played like I've spent all season hoping they would, like I know they can.

Maybe, just maybe, I'm reading too much into my contribution. Perhaps the Frenchmen in the team thought their point was to prove themselves to the nine non-French players in the squad. But I don't think so. I prefer to be positive, to think I got through to everyone in our team — those of us who've been invited to come and play rugby in this country and also those who were born here. Although it's taken almost all this season, I think I managed to find and push the button that makes the French tick. *Je l'espère. I hope so.*

The 2005–2006 season is shaping up to be a huge one for Castres Olympique. It will be our centenary season and the club hierarchy have made no secret that what they covet most is the French championship title and possibly the European Cup. Now that would give them a season they could talk about for a long time! It will be real champagne rugby if we can achieve those goals.

Because of the centenary, there is a lot of talk that the club has the chequebook out and is giving incoming coach Laurent Seigne carte-blanche to draw up a shopping list so that he can go out and recruit the players he deems necessary for the club to realise its ambitions. His reputation may be that of a hard task-master but many consider him to be the best forwards' coach in France. He'll get nothing but support from me as he strives to improve the standard of the club on and off the pitch and I'm looking forward to his arrival.

Apparently, Laurent will not be arriving here alone. He's reported to be bringing his medical staff with him, which signifies a real changing of the guard. Such a move can only benefit the team, mentally and physically. Knowing that any injuries are going to be properly diagnosed and dealt with promptly will go a long way to restoring the team's faith in matters medical, and no one will miss those onerous trips to Toulouse to receive treatment.

If Castres is to be challenging consistently for a top-four spot in the French championship it needs to adopt a much more professional approach to all areas of the club: players, coaches, support staff and management. Laurent Seigne's appointment is an indication that things are moving in the right direction to achieve that goal. Divisions caused by cultural and language differences and difficulties are areas he seems keen to address and apparently he is planning to implement French classes each day after training. They will be compulsory and I am certain that, as a team, if we are all able to better understand and speak French it will go a long way to improving team morale and our on-the-field performances. Gesticulation can only get you so far, and if we can improve our communication skills it can only have a positive impact on the way we play.

Hopefully, Laurent possesses the ability to harness and develop the rugby talent at his disposal. At times during this season we've promised much but never seriously threatened to break into the top four and therefore be in contention for the playoffs to decide *le championnat*. Mostly, we've held the fifth spot but as the season's progressed we've dipped to sixth.

Even after the big win against Montferrand we remain rooted to the sixth spot. It's vital we don't fall any further because that would take us out of the Heineken Cup competition. But with only three games to go it looks likely we'll be safe for a place in Europe next season.

One of the biggest problems with French rugby is the huge movement of players every season and the consequent lack of consistency is impacting negatively on a lot of clubs. A more stable player pool would be of huge benefit to clubs such as Castres.

You need look no further than two of New Zealand's best-performing sides, Canterbury and my old stamping ground of Otago, to see what consistency — among players and coaching staff — can do for you. The abilities of these two provinces to continually develop, without ever ringing huge changes among their players, has kept them near or at the top of the game in New Zealand.

It's quite a different story with Auckland who can be top of the table one year and down near the bottom the next. While I don't wish to bag my former province, I see similarities between what is happening in France and what has occurred in Auckland. In my opinion, it's not the way forward.

And if the French ever decide to become properly professional then, as I've said before . . . watch out world!

Revoir en esprit. To look back on. When I look back over my first season at Castres I see many positives. Sure, there have been frustrations on and off the field, but nothing insurmountable. If the first season is, as everyone keeps telling me, the most difficult and challenging, they have nothing but good things to say about the second, and how enjoyable and easier it will be.

What have I enjoyed most? Rugby-wise it would have to be the game against Toulouse. They're a big, top-flight club and when, months ago, they showed an interest in me of course I was keen. But they stuffed me around and ended up signing another prop. After that debacle I signed with Castres.

I hadn't been at Castres very long; in fact I was playing only my third game for them when we met the mighty Toulouse. I felt I had a point to prove (did I mention before that I'm rather competitive by nature?) and we dominated the scrum so much that they, in my opinion, faked an injury to two of their props so that the scrums became non-contested. And, of course, we won the match. Point well and truly proved, I'd say.

Then, in our game against Brive I really felt as though I'd come to grips with, not only my positional play, but also my around-the-field play. I was in the right places at the right times, which meant I was then able to play the ball-in-hand game I'm used to.

That Castres is a truly multi-national side has given me the opportunity to play alongside guys from so many different countries and to learn about them and their cultures. It's been a wonderful experience, school-of-life stuff, and something else I have rugby to thank for.

As for the lifestyle, it's been nothing but fantastic for my family and me. Not only have we made friends among expat team-mates and their families but we now have a group of warm, friendly and hospitable French friends. Anywhere you go you meet some people you click instantly with, and then there are others who take a while longer to get to know well, where you go through more of what I like to refer to as the 'polite' phase.

Le Rugbyman

We clicked instantly with Laurence and Bruno and also with Jacques and Christy, the owners of the restaurant *La Grillade* that we happily frequent.

Jacques and Christy are quite a bit older than Juanita and me — they'd be more in the 'young grandparent' category — but the age difference has proved no barrier to the four of us forming a good friendship. Just two weekends ago we spent a leisurely day enjoying lunch at their beautiful country home complete with its marquee, swimming pool and expansive garden. We got to enjoy more of Jacques' wonderful cooking. On this occasion he created cuisine *à la Maroque* (Moroccan), and there we were — 20 of us in total — talking, drinking and eating al fresco at long white wooden tables. Then, when the sun got too hot we were forced to test the temperature of his swimming pool. It paints a perfect picture, doesn't it? Yeah, well, it's just one of the delights about living here — the hospitality of the people.

I'm sorry to say but that's exactly what it's like. I cannot tell a lie. It's difficult, almost impossible to do justice to it via these pages. You know those movies or books *Under the Tuscan Sun*, *Chocolat*, *Stealing Beauty* or even *Captain Corelli's Mandolin*? To us, that's what our life is like — and more. We feel blessed.

Juanita's grandfather, the late great Eric Steel, often said: 'It is the people who make a place. You could live in the biggest city in the world and be as lonely as hell; you could also live in the smallest town and not be lonely at all.'

I get his point entirely. We seem a million miles from home, and for a time didn't really know anyone here. But that Castres is a small town is to its — and our — benefit. There's a real feeling of community, and as I stroll the streets I see familiar faces and I feel

Season's End

part of the place. It's this familiarity that I look forward to when I return from traipsing around the country, or other countries for that matter. Castres is now the place I'm talking about when I say, 'I can't wait to get home.' I'm grateful this town chose me to represent them. It's definitely people who make or break a place and I'm really enjoying getting to know the locals.

If we love the people, we're just as enamoured with the French culture. There is so much about the place to admire, and not just their wine, food, pretty towns and even their furniture. It's about everyday things — such as siesta time.

It's the time of day I've come to cherish. At first, fresh off the plane from New Zealand, I thought it was most inconvenient of the shops, the banks or even the dry-cleaners to close their doors from midday until 2.30 pm. After all, I had to be at training for 3 pm. What if I needed to go out and buy something?

But now I see it differently. I welcome the rest, and instead of racing round trying to do chores I get to enjoy a leisurely lunch either at home or in a restaurant, and as the weather warms up Juanita, the girls and I can take our midday meal to the great outdoors and have picnics. The local lakes are inviting and not too far from our place and we have a national park on our doorstep, almost literally, because it is only two kilometres up the road. I enjoy visiting the park, it gives me my nature fix, and I get to listen to the birds singing, something I always loved about New Zealand.

That Sunday is quite literally a day of rest has also been a huge bonus. France is almost a closed shop on Sundays. The patisserie will be open until lunchtime and you can buy your paper from the *tabac*, but apart from that shopping as we've become used to it in New Zealand doesn't exist in France.

Le Rugbyman

If we want big-city life or a trip to the ocean, we don't have far to travel. And talking of travel, we've been fortunate with our sightseeing adventures to date. I've only begun to scratch the surface of my long list of 'must-go there' and 'must-see that', but what fun we've had planning and visiting different places and countries.

But the biggest gain since coming to France has been about time. Having *more* time. I miss my family when I have to go away for one or two nights, but then I stop for a minute and look back on my life in New Zealand. How did we cope back then with having to spend virtually three months apart during various All Black seasons? It's hard to remember but I know it wasn't fun.

Now, I get to spend time with my babies. I've been there to witness all their milestones and getting to know them as little people. It's an experience I find impossible to articulate. I adore my girls and that I'm able to spend so much time with them, to enjoy everyday activities and to live a normal family life, means more to me than anything.

Of course, living in France means I'm not as involved in the lives of my three children back in New Zealand. I miss them like crazy and being so far away from them is the major downside to living here.

Are there any other lowlights? Being an optimist by nature, I can't think of anything too terrible. Sure there's been the haunted house, having nowhere to live for a while, and the hiring and firing of coaches. But I put all those things down to experience. In fact, when I look back and relive most of the incidents I find myself laughing about them. They make for great yarns.

There have been difficulties naturally and the language would be one of the major obstacles to overcome. But it's also what living in a foreign country is all about, that and having to come

Season's End

to terms with cultural and work environment differences. Most of the time I've managed to roll with the punches, so to speak, and got by with nothing more serious than a few scrapes and the occasional whinge.

Yes . . . the occasional whinge. Perhaps you're wondering where my stories are of what *really* happened behind the scenes of All Black, Otago and Auckland rugby? Quite frankly, I didn't want to write about any of that. Sure, many interesting things happened during those days but they're in the past.

During those years there were occasions when I wanted to shout out loud about what was going on, to let the public know the real truth. But, taking a deep breath can also be a good thing, and when I look back none of those events which at the time seemed monumental affected me greatly. These days I can reflect on events that once infuriated or upset me and feel a sense of satisfaction in knowing that I came through those testing times and actually learned something from them — without letting it all hang out!

Do I miss New Zealand rugby? I do. Just that — the rugby and the style of play and the speed at which it's played. However, my time here has been more than fulfilling enough to keep at bay any second thoughts I may have had about walking away from the All Blacks. I'm continually learning more about front-row play, and meeting the challenge of being as good a prop here as I was in New Zealand and on the international rugby stage, keeps me driven.

But would I do it again? Would I walk away from the All Blacks and into a rugby team that's a sometimes crazy mix of Frenchmen, Argentineans, English, Irish and New Zealanders, coached by an equally volatile group of men and with an ambitious and cut-throat club management?

Picture this. It's the month of May and at that time every year since 1999 (the year after I was first selected for the All Blacks) I'd have been stressed out and wondering if I was good enough to make All Black selection that season. Questions would race through my mind. Was my Super 12 season good enough? Have I done enough to secure my position in the squad? What will we do if I'm not selected? Will we be able to pay the mortgage? Am I a peacock or a feather duster?

You'd find out your fate at the same time as the rest of New Zealand. Usually, Juanita and I would be sitting by the TV, waiting, anticipating, full of anxiety and hoping that my name would be called (you were never quite certain what the coach was looking for when compiling his team). Then the overwhelming relief when you heard your name read out.

I'm glad those days are over and that my immediate future is certain. This is the first time in my life when I've been able to plan for my future and to a large extent have some control over it. Would I do it again? *Bien sûr. Of course.*

About the Writer

HEATHER KIDD is a former assistant editor of *Rugby News* and was New Zealand Sports Writer of the Year in 1990. She is well qualified to work with Kees Meeuws on his book, having lived in France for five years with her husband Murray, a player and later coach of *Lyon Olympique Universitaire*.

After nearly 20 years writing about rugby, and while living in Cork, in Ireland, Heather wrote general sports features and worked as a sub-editor for the *Irish Examiner*. Returning to New Zealand in 2003 after almost 13 years living abroad, Heather is based in Auckland where she is chief sub-editor for *Next* magazine.